NATHANIEL LACHENMEYER is the author of the award-winning *The Outsider: A Journey into My Father's Struggle with Madness,* as well as several children's books. He lives on Long Island.

13 FACTS ABOUT 13

1

Contrary to popular opinion, Friday the 13th emerged as a superstition only in the early twentieth century.

2

Continental, Air France, and Lufthansa omit the 13th row on their planes—the sequence jumps from Row 12 to Row 14.

3

The original title of the film *Friday the 13th* was *Long Night at Camp Blood.* It was renamed to imitate the successful formula of the calendar-driven film *Halloween* (1978).

4

The Waldorf-Astoria is one of the only New York hotels with a 13th floor.

5

Triskaidekaphobia can be treated by behavioral therapy: for example, getting a triskaidekaphobe to visit the 13th floor of a building and spend more and more time there.

6

The Thirteen Club dined on lobster salad in the shape of coffins.

7

Some conspiracies state that the McDonald's logo is a 13. Others that the patterns of 13 on the American dollar bill act as a protective force over the United States.

8

13 is not unlucky in the Far East. In China, Taiwan, Japan, and Korea the number 4 is extremely unlucky.

9

Australian Cricket players call 87 "the devil's number," as it is 13 short of 100.

10

In the United States 13 used to be considered particularly benevolent, as it was the original number of colonies that united to gain independence from Britain.

11

Tuesday the 13th is unlucky in Latin countries.

12

Other very unlucky numbers in Western culture are 666, the number of the beast in Revelations, and 3—hence "bad things always come in 3s."

13

On Friday, October 13, 1989, the Dow Jones suffered its second biggest points drop since Black Monday in 1987. On that occasion some traders connected the huge fall with the fact there had been three Friday the 13ths that year.

NATHANIEL LACHENMEYER

13

THE STORY OF
THE WORLD'S MOST NOTORIOUS SUPERSTITION

A PLUME BOOK

For Arlo, who makes his parents feel lucky every day

PLUME
Published by Penguin Group
Penguin Group (USA) Inc., 375 Hudson Street, New York, New York 10014, U.S.A.
Penguin Group (Canada), 90 Eglinton Avenue East, Suite 700, Toronto, Ontario,
Canada M4P 2Y3 (a division of Pearson Penguin Canada Inc.)
Penguin Books Ltd., 80 Strand, London WC2R 0RL, England
Penguin Ireland, 25 St. Stephen's Green, Dublin 2, Ireland
(a division of Penguin Books Ltd.)
Penguin Group (Australia), 250 Camberwell Road, Camberwell, Victoria 3124,
Australia (a division of Pearson Australia Group Pty. Ltd.)
Penguin Books India Pvt. Ltd., 11 Community Centre, Panchsheel Park,
New Delhi – 110 017, India
Penguin Books (NZ), cnr Airborne and Rosedale Roads, Albany, Auckland 1310,
New Zealand (a division of Pearson New Zealand Ltd.)
Penguin Books (South Africa) (Pty.) Ltd., 24 Sturdee Avenue, Rosebank,
Johannesburg 2196, South Africa

Penguin Books Ltd., Registered Offices: 80 Strand, London WC2R 0RL, England

Published by Plume, a member of Penguin Group (USA) Inc. This is an authorized reprint
of a hardcover edition published by Thunder's Mouth Press. For information address
Thunder's Mouth Press, 245 West 17th Street, 11th Floor, New York, New York 10011.

First Plume Printing, September 2005
10   9   8   7   6   5   4   3   2   1

Unless otherwise noted, illustrations are courtesy of the General Research Division,
the New York Public Library.

Ⓟ REGISTERED TRADEMARK—MARCA REGISTRADA

CIP data is available
ISBN 1-56858-306-0 (hc.)
ISBN 0-452-28496-1 (pbk.)

Printed in the United States of America

Contents

The superstitions about Friday and 13 were once believed by those reputed wise; now such men regard them as harmless follies. But probably...years hence many beliefs of the wise of our day will come to seem equally foolish. Man is a credulous animal, and must believe *something*; in the absence of good grounds for belief, he will be satisfied with bad ones.

—Bertrand Russell, *Unpopular Essays* (1950)

13 SUPERSTITIONS ABOUT 13

1

Thirteen is an unlucky number.

2

If 13 people sit at a table, one will die within a year.*

3

The 13th day of the month is unlucky.

4

Friday the 13th is an unlucky day.**

5

It is unlucky to start a journey on the 13th.

6

The 13th floor is unlucky.

7

Room No. 13 is unlucky.

8

It is unlucky to have the number 13 in your street address.

*More 13-at-a-table superstitions can be found on page 4.
**More Friday the 13th superstitions can be found on page 84.

9

Thirteen steps lead to bad luck.

10

A clock striking 13 portends a death in the family.

11

It is unlucky to have 13 letters in your name.

12

Numbers that add up to 13 are unlucky (e.g., 454).

13

It is unlucky to have 13 coins in your pocket.

Preface

T HE BOOK WAS covered in torn and stained brown paper—
a handmade dust jacket ravaged by time. On the spine,
barely visible in faded ink, was the abbreviation, *No. 21.*
Underneath it, a single word: *Miscellany.* When I opened it, I was
surprised to discover that it was a scrapbook: Newspaper clippings had been glued onto every page, completely covering the
original text. Reinforced with clippings and glue on both sides,
the pages were stiff and warped. True to the title, the clippings
seemed to be included at random—evidently, these were the articles that had caught the attention of the owner but didn't fit into
books 1–20. Most of the articles were from 1860 to 1900,

although a few dated back as far as the 1830s. The headlines were intriguing: AMERICAN VOLCANOES; THE SENSATION OF HALF A CENTURY AGO / MURDER OF SARAH M. CORNELL; SUPERSTITIONS ABOUT HAIR; ORIGIN OF BLIND MAN'S BLUFF; ALAS, POOR GHOST! MRS. ROBERT I. HULL'S "MATERIALIZATIONS" EXPOSED; THE WOOD ISLAND TRAGEDY; A GREAT OUTRAGE / THE BODY OF ALEXANDER T. STEWART STOLEN; A SKELETON IN EVERY HOUSE; SEVEN MOUNTAINS OF FLESH. . . .

Walking up to the counter of the roadside antique store with my prize in hand, I promised myself that when I got home I would read the scrapbook cover to cover, treating it like a book. Three years later, I still haven't achieved that goal. But I do pick it up from time to time and allow myself a quick glance at the news. The odds are still better than 50-50 that I'll find an article I haven't read yet. It was at just such a moment that I discovered the article about the Thirteen Club.

WRECKED BY DYNAMITE.

The " Thirteen Club" Blown Up and Three Hurt.

WOODBURY, N. J., March 18.—The house of the " Thirteen Club," on the creek, was wrecked last night with dynamite which was placed under the building. The windows were blown out, the floors ripped up, and the entire place made a wreck. Three members were in the clubhouse at the time and were thrown some distance, but escaped with a few bruises.

There is no clue to the fiends. A man went by the house in a boat a few minutes before the explosion and is presumed to be the guilty party. No reason is known for the act.

I had never heard of the Thirteen Club. I was curious about what it was and why someone would want to blow it up. I turned the page, expecting to find an article on a completely different subject—a gruesome murder or a new miracle cure for a disease

we don't have anymore—but I was wrong. On the next page were
more Thirteen Club headlines: DEFYING OLD SUPERSTITIONS;
THIRTEEN AT TABLE. I turned the page again: THIRTEEN CLUB MEM-
BER'S DEATH; THIRTEEN CLUB HERESY TRIAL. In all, the scrapbook
contained eleven articles on the Thirteen Club, all dating from
1885 to 1899. I was intrigued; it was the first time I had found anything in *Miscellany* that suggested a pattern. Up until that point,
the only facts I had been able to surmise about the creator of the
scrapbook were that he was from the Northeast—most of the
articles were from Northeast papers—and that he probably was a
"he." (Tucked into the scrapbook was a folded advertisement
from a Victorian era men's clothier that offered men's heavy rid-
ing ulsters, sack suits, boy's knee pant suits, reefers, spring over-
sacks, and kilt suits.) Although the collection of articles on the
Thirteen Club didn't add anything to what I knew already, it did
introduce an interesting possibility: Was the creator of *Miscellany*
a member of the Thirteen Club? There is no way to know—but I
like to think that he was.

CHAPTER ONE

The Thirteen Club

"With malice toward none and charity to all," we have invited every race and creed to join our movement, and render their aid in crushing an evil not advocated by any class, but injurious to all alike.

—Chief Ruler David McAdam,
Thirteen Club Annual Address (January 13, 1890)

I HAD NEVER HEARD of the 13-at-a-table superstition until I read the Thirteen Club articles in *Miscellany*. For most of the nineteenth century, unlucky 13 at a table was the most popular superstition in the world. The most common variation of the superstition was that if 13 people sat together at a table, one would die within a year. There was a general consensus at the time that 13 at a table was the original 13 superstition, and that it was inspired by the fateful events of the Last Supper: Christ and his twelve disciples sat down at a table; the next day Christ was crucified. His betrayer, Judas Iscariot, one of the twelve, also died. The precise interpretation of the superstition varied: Some people believed that 13's bad luck reflected the fate of Christ; others, that of Judas. Most assumed that 13 at a table had existed since that fateful day and had always been popular. However, it was only in the nineteenth century that newspapers began regaling readers with anecdotes about dinner parties being broken up by the late discovery of an unlucky 13th guest, and that magazines frequently featured ghost stories and mysteries that drew on unlucky 13. With each passing decade, there were more and more references to the superstition. Nor were private correspondence and diaries exempt from this trend. Especially after mid-century, everyone, it seemed, knew someone who had sat at a table of 13 where someone had died within a year. By the 1860s, awareness of unlucky 13 was so pervasive that a person with a run of 13s in his life had to have a position on the subject: Was 13 unlucky, lucky, or neither?

In the 1880s a group of influential New Yorkers decided that enough was enough, and set out to put an end to the superstition. The person who spearheaded the effort was Captain William Fowler, a well-known Civil War veteran and man-about-town. Years later, in his obituary, the *New York Times* recalled, "Every 'good liver' of fifteen or twenty years ago knew Capt. Fowler, and associated with his name good fellowship, a big heart, and simple unostentatious charity." Captain Fowler's interest in 13 sprang from a series of coincidences in his own life involving the number. He participated in 13 major battles in the Civil War; he was forced to resign his commission on August 13, 1863, after having been wounded; and on the 13th of the following month, he purchased the Knickerbocker Cottage on Sixth Avenue near 28th Street, which quickly became a popular meeting place for local social clubs and organizations. Fowler's connection to 13 did not end there; in an era in which membership in clubs determined a man's social standing, Fowler belonged to 13 of the best of them.

In 1880, Captain Fowler threw down the gauntlet to fate. His plan was simple: to start a new social club where members would meet for dinner on the 13th of each month and sit 13 to a table. They would challenge 13 to make good on its threat that if 13 people sat at a table, one would die within a year. Unlike other 13 superstitions, 13 at a table had the advantage of being empirically testable: If everyone survived the year, the superstition was a bust; if someone died, and the subjects were willing to continue, the experiment could be repeated to rule out chance.

It took Fowler a year to find 13 people brave enough to join his club. The inaugural dinner of the Thirteen Club took place at 8:13 P.M. on Friday, January 13, 1881, in Room 13 of the Knickerbocker Cottage. From the beginning, it was a calculated attack not just on 13, but on all the popular superstitions of the day. Members had to walk under a ladder to reach the table set for 13; once there, they were met with piles of spilled salt and forks crossed at each place setting. The Thirteen Clubbers were rationalists who saw superstition as a relic of the past that impeded progress. Nonetheless, even the twelve "good livers" who joined Fowler that night may have been given pause when, upon arrival, they were confronted with an enormous white-on-red banner that read "*Morituri Te Salutamus*" ("We who are about to die salute you"). The dinner was as pleasantly uneventful as anyone could have hoped: good conversation, good food, and no one suddenly falling face-first into his dessert.

VARIATIONS ON A THEME:
13 SUPERSTITIONS ABOUT 13 AT A TABLE

1

If 13 people sit together at a table, one will die within a year.

2

If 13 people sit down at a table,
the last to sit down will die first.

3

If 13 people sit down to a meal,
the first to rise from the table will die.

4

If 13 people sit at a dinner table,
the first and the last to leave will die soon.

5

If 13 people sit at a table, everyone must rise at once,
or the first to rise will die within a year.

6

If 13 people find themselves seated at a table,
they can avert death by joining hands and rising as one.

7

If you serve 13 people at the table, the youngest will die.

8

If you set a table with 13 places, one of the guests will die.

9

If someone sneezes at a table where 13 people are sitting,
the oldest or the youngest will die within the year.

10

Never have 13 guests to dinner because
one of the guests will die before dawn.

11

If 13 people sit together at a dinner table, there will be
a death in the host's family during the coming year.

12

If 13 people sit at a table, one will get food poisoning.

13

Don't sit 13 people at a table on Friday or one will become ill;
on Friday the 13th, one will become seriously ill.

Captain Fowler's sense of theatrics and gift for self-promotion made the Thirteen Club a success from the start. Two months after its inception, there were already enough members to fill two tables of 13 in Room 13 of the Knickerbocker Cottage. Fowler had hit on a brilliant strategy to extend the club's reach and garner publicity: He sent letters inviting influential New Yorkers to become *honorary* Thirteen Club members—members who didn't actually have to sit at a table of 13 (and risk premature death), but only lend their support by return letter. The strategy paid off: On March 14, 1882, the Thirteen Club's third dinner made it into the *New York Times*. The article ended with an impressive list of honorary members who were elected in absentia, including two judges, two state senators, two coroners, the county clerk, the public works commissioner, the excise commissioner, and the president of the ASPCA. Fowler did nothing by halves; he also courted national figures as potential honorary members, starting at the top. The 13th acceptance letter read aloud at the dinner was from the new president of the United States, Chester A. Arthur. The *Times* article heralded the beginning of a long, mutually beneficial relationship between the club and the paper that resulted in dozens of articles over the next two decades.

The Thirteen Club quickly came into its own as one of New York's most illustrious social clubs. The mainstay of the club's monthly meeting was a marathon series of speeches about superstition by members and invited guests—a mix of earnest analysis and broad satire. The macabre emphasis on 13 and death hinted at in the first club dinner became more elaborate. Most dinners featured menus in the shape of tombstones and skull candlestick holders. One month, members were served large platters of lobster salad that had been molded into the shape of coffins; on top of each was a miniature coffin plate embossed with the number 13. Another month the dessert was a large cake decorated with 13 lilacs—an allusion to Walt Whitman's famous elegy to Lincoln, "When Lilacs Last in the Dooryard Bloom'd." At one dinner, the club hosted 13 undertakers at their very own table of 13. Other superstitions were always targeted in addition to the mortal fear of 13; open umbrellas, broken mirrors, and silhouettes of black cats were standard decor at many dinners.

The Thirteen Club grew at an extraordinary rate: There were 13 new members in 1882, 325 in 1883, 147 in 1884, 263 in 1885, 119 in 1886, and 487 in 1887—its banner year. On August 13, 1886, Thirteen Club members converged on Coney Island for the fifty-fifth dinner of the original Thirteen Club and the fourth annual "feast by the sea"—a midsummer banquet to which representatives from every Thirteen Club were invited. The event was attended by 338 Thirteen Clubbers (twenty-six tables of 13 each); including guests, nearly 400 people joined in the celebration.

By the mid-1880s, Thirteen Clubs had sprung up around the country. Some were official "branch clubs" of the New York Thirteen Club—the charter cost thirteen dollars plus thirteen cents per month payable as dues. There were branch clubs in Illinois, Michigan, Pennsylvania, Connecticut, and New Jersey, as well as four additional New York branches. There were also other "unofficial" Thirteen Clubs in the United States and abroad that were inspired by the newspaper coverage of the original, but did not pay dues. Outside the United States, there were

Thirteen Clubs as far north as Nova Scotia and as far south as Chile. The phenomenon even crossed the Atlantic. An 1885 article in the *London Daily News* reported that "even here there is a little coterie of 13 men who dine together monthly at a house numbered 13 and pay 13s. each for their dinner and 13d. to each of the waiters." The article, however, predicted that despite its rapid growth and international popularity, the Thirteen Club would fail in its mission: "still the superstition is as lively as of yore all over Europe and America, and probably it will continue to flourish and make people uncomfortable until the end of time."

The chief rulers of the Thirteen Club in its first decade included two of New York's most prominent men: David McAdam, chief justice of the City Court, and Michael J. B. Messemer, New York City coroner. (Captain Fowler was the club's permanent custodian–master of ceremonies.) In 1892, Messemer yielded the reins to John H. V. Arnold, onetime acting mayor of New York, president of the Democratic Club, president of the Board of Aldermen, and soon-to-be head of the Surrogate's Court of the county of New York, which had jurisdiction over the probate of wills and testaments and the settlement of estates. Arnold was known for his hobbies: he had one of the best private collections of autographs in the country, and he was one of the era's best-known book collectors (at a time when a rare-book collection transferred to its owner both prestige and a unique store of knowledge). He also had a talent for litterateurs, or "extra illustration"—the once-popular practice of interleaving old books with new pages to supplement the information they contained. When I discovered Arnold's pastime, it occurred to me that *Miscellany* might be a relic from his library, although I suspected that if it were, he would not have condemned the Thirteen Club to *Miscellany* or stopped at eleven articles.

The Thirteen Club continued to grow in its second decade. On January 13, 1892, the occasion of its tenth anniversary and hundredth dinner, the club claimed a thousand members. Members from this period included some of the most interesting men of the day. The eccentric George Francis Train was a onetime presidential candidate who had helped secure financing for three major railroad companies, set a record for the fastest trip around the world, and had twice been subjected to public hearings questioning his sanity. Thomas Dunn English was in his lifetime a doctor, a lawyer, and a congressman, but he was most beloved as the composer of the popular song "Ben Bolt." Famed bandleader and trombone player Carlo Alberto Cappa was an enthusiastic member, and he often included a club-inspired tune, "The Thirteen Club Galop," in his public performances. General Horatio C. King, toastmaster of the Thirteen Club during this period, was one of the most decorated soldiers of the Civil War, a respected lawyer, the former editor of the *New York Star*, and the publisher of *The Christian Union* and *The Christian at Work*. Henry Romeike was the inventor of the press clippings bureau, an early database that allowed the newsworthy to find out what the world's papers had to say about them. It was Romeike who was responsible for collecting the newspaper coverage of the Thirteen Club that was featured in the club's annual reports. Given his penchant for newspaper clippings, Romeike was another possible candidate for the creator of *Miscellany*, but its lack of organization would have been anathema to someone whose livelihood depended on his ability to locate and retrieve information efficiently.

In the 1890s, the Thirteen Club ushered in a new era of social clubs. At the time there was a nearly universal belief (at least among men) that women were the more superstitious sex and that their influence around the hearth played a significant role in keeping superstitions alive. The Thirteen Club was convinced that in order to eradicate superstition, it had to reach out to women. The club's movement in this direction began in 1891 with a "ladies' reception." While a handful of New York clubs had provisions allowing members' wives and daughters to visit under prescribed conditions, in general social clubs were the exclusive domain of men. The prospect of enlivening a Thirteen Club dinner with the presence of ladies inspired members to make the setting especially ghoulish. The *New York Times* reported: "Each fair guest will find a miniature glass coffin at her plate, and, if she has courage enough to lift the lid and take a last look at the contents, she will discover therein a tiny bottle of perfume, the stopper a tolerably accurate representation of a human skull." In keeping with their progressive agenda, the club also invited suffragists to speak on several occasions. The suffragists embraced the Thirteen Club and used it as a platform for discussing the "superstitions" that continued to encourage women's subjugation, including the belief that every woman was the temptress Eve. The club soon went beyond receptions and guest lectures. At a time when women's clubs were still a new and radical idea, the Thirteen Club encouraged the formation of separate Thirteen Clubs for women. Due in part to the efforts of the Thirteen Club, women's clubs emerged as a social force during this period.

In addition to the arrival of women's clubs, there was an explosion of novelty clubs in the 1890s, many of which drew their inspiration from the Thirteen Club. New Yorkers could choose between the Morgue Club (a copycat Thirteen Club), the Ghost Club (people who had encountered ghosts), the Liars' Club (a collection of boastful fishermen), the Impecunious Club (wealthy penny-pinchers), the Five-Pounders (gluttons who swore not to leave the table until they had gained five pounds), the Suicide Club (members swore to die by their own hands rather than leave their exit to fate), and so on. Many of these clubs made use of the kinds of irreverent rituals and set pieces that the Thirteen Club had pioneered a decade earlier. Bringing his satirical gift to bear on the proliferation of clubs, Captain William Fowler also founded a new club during this period: he called it the Club of Two. Its members consisted of himself and a friend, and they agreed to take turns being president.

Ironically, the wave of new social clubs in the 1890s resulted in increased competition for members and led to a drop in Thirteen Clubbers. The membership rolls were also hurt by rumors that the Thirteen Club was itself a suicide club. In an effort to dispel them, Captain Fowler reported at the 13th annual dinner in 1895 that the suicide rate for Thirteen Clubbers was actually lower than that of the general population, and that out of the 2,542 members who had joined the club since its inception, "the total death list was but 122." But two years later, in 1897, the club reported only 626 members, a decline of 37 percent from

1892. That same year, Captain William Fowler died, signaling the end of an era. The old guard, which had managed to keep death at bay long enough to prove that 13 at a table wasn't fatal, was now proving that life itself was. By the end of the decade, a reader of the *New York Times* was as likely to find a reference to the Thirteen Club in the obituaries as they were to read an article about the club's latest dinner.

Three members who were lucky to stay out of the obituaries in 1898 were the unnamed men who were in the Thirteen Club in Woodbury, New Jersey, when it was blown up—the subject of the first Thirteen Club article I came across in *Miscellany*. There was no follow-up in the *New York Times* on the Thirteen Club bomber; apparently, he escaped justice. Now that I knew more about the club, it occurred to me that he may have been a militant triskaidekaphobe who was sick of the club mocking his beliefs. Someone who had grown exasperated with members' immunity to the 13-at-a-table superstition and decided to help fate along. In those frenzied triskaidekaphobic times, it did not seem impossible. In 1903, an article in the *New York Times* entitled "Origin of Common Superstitions" confirmed that the superstition was as pervasive as ever:

> No thoughtful hostess to-day, however much she disbelieves in this idea herself, will unite thirteen people at table for fear of making some one uncomfortable.... Who cannot recall in his own experience some occasion in which some one (a child perhaps) was pressed into service to swell the number to fourteen? Or when some luckless

child, who had looked forward to a feast with "grown-ups," had to leave the table, a victim on the altar of this insane superstition?

Three years later, the Thirteen Club annual report recorded a total of 339 active members—after subtracting 10 resignations, 16 suspensions, and 7 deaths. The average dinner attendance that year was 236 members. Although past its prime, the Thirteen Club still had connections and influence. Chester Arthur was the first U.S. president to become an honorary member of the Thirteen Club, but he would not be the last. On April 13, 1907, the club traveled en masse to Washington and met with honorary member Theodore Roosevelt. According to the club's annual report, "A miniature teddy bear was presented to the Chief Executive of the nation by the Chief Executive of the Thirteen Club, or, as the programme expressed it, from one Chief Ruler to another Chief Ruler." Over the course of its history, the Thirteen Club claimed five successive U.S. presidents as honorary members: Chester Arthur, Grover Cleveland, Benjamin Harrison, William McKinley, and Theodore Roosevelt.

If the Thirteen Club was no closer to achieving its goals in the new century than it had been in 1881, at least its tactics were as inventive as ever. An elaborate new antisuperstition tradition had emerged to supplement the marathon speechmaking at Thirteen Club dinners: mock trials. At each trial, members were assigned the roles of jury, attorneys, witnesses, and defendant. The defendant was accused of indulging in a popular superstition, such as attending a séance or throwing a pinch of salt over his left shoulder after knocking over the saltshaker. Over the course of the evening, the defendant was tried and invariably convicted for his foolishness. The Thirteen Club continued to strive to add imaginative set pieces to the decor. The thirtieth annual dinner of the Thirteen Club on February 13, 1911, brought a new innovation: an electric "13" sign. For the occasion, the club turned off its electric chandeliers and lit a candle at each table setting to combat the superstition that it was unlucky to eat by candlelight. This, of course, was a recent superstition; it would not have been considered unlucky to eat by candlelight when candles were the main source of illumination. Even during the Thirteen Club's heyday, there were greater forces at work when it came to ending a superstition—among them, changes in technology. Back in 1887, the club had flouted a very different candle superstition: if people were sitting at a table illuminated by candles and someone's candle went out, that person would be the first to die. A very short candle was placed in front of each club member to guarantee that one of the candles would go out before the night was over. This superstition became extinct with electric light's conquest of the candle.

By the second decade of the twentieth century, fewer and fewer articles on the Thirteen Club were finding their way into print. Even the club's perennial champion, the *New York Times*, was losing interest. In 1917, the *Times* ran what was by then a rare article covering a club dinner—"13-Cent Tips by Thirteen Club." The host of the dinner was chief ruler Colonel John F. Hobbes, who had also been chief ruler in 1907—he presented President Roosevelt with the teddy bear. Colonel Hobbes was one of the most colorful members in the club's history. He was the editor and publisher of two hotel trade papers and the commissioner of city revenue—but according to contemporary newspaper accounts, he was also a king. In 1890, he had been shipwrecked on one of the New Hebrides islands near Australia. Hobbes not only survived his first encounters with the natives, he lived among them and taught them Western war craft, which helped them defeat a neighboring tribe. Out of gratitude, they made him king. Hobbes's kingdom consisted of four islands with a combined population of 35,000. One of his first official acts was to abolish cannibalism. Hobbes returned to the U.S. in 1893. Although he never revisited his kingdom, he retained the title until his death in 1928. Given the Thirteen Club's illustrious history, it is fitting that one of its last chief rulers was a king.

The last appearance of the Thirteen Club in the *New York Times* is a brief announcement of the forty-first annual dinner, which appeared in the column "In the Current Week" on December 9, 1923. After that, there is nothing. The only account I was able to find of the club's demise was written by J. Arthur Lehman, who was chief ruler of the Thirteen Club in 1913. Unfortunately, however, Lehman seems to have gotten his facts wrong. On Friday, March 13, 1936, the United Press carried a story in which Lehman revisited the club's glory days. The former chief ruler claimed that the Thirteen Club officially disbanded in 1914 because with the advent of World War I the club's hallmark irreverence toward death no longer seemed appropriate or in keeping with the times. Right or wrong, more than two decades later, Lehman was still a Thirteen Clubber at heart: "My advice to anyone that wants real luck and happiness and health is to break every possible known superstition today. . . . All the members of the club that I can remember had good luck. . . . I'm 78 now and I defy you to find anyone happier or healthier than I am.

Thirteen Clubs outside New York outlasted the club that inspired them, although in many cases the connection to the original was forgotten over time. As of 1933, there was still a Thirteen Club in Duquesne, Pennsylvania. As late as 1940, there was a Thirteen Club in Washington, D.C. Women's Thirteen Clubs and collegiate Thirteen Clubs also survived the original club. Lectures presented by Women's Thirteen Clubs were included in the *New York Times*'s regular listing of activities for "clubwomen" into the 1930s. In the 1930s, there were still Thirteen Clubs at both the College of William and Mary and Washington and Lee University. Between 1921 and 1943, there was a Thirteen Club at the University of North Carolina, Chapel Hill.

During the 1940s, Thirteen Clubs served as key plot devices in at least two mystery novels: the impressively unreadable *No Past Is Dead* by J. J. Connington, in which the first corpse is discovered being gnawed on by a pet cheetah; and *13 Toy Pistols* by E. E. Halleran, an entertaining combination of hard-boiled and drawing-room mystery. A Thirteen Club was even featured in a *Batman* comic book from 1947; the cover shows a ladder, a bucket of paint, and a mirror falling on the Joker as Batman, Robin, and a black cat look on and laugh; a newspaper headline reveals that it is Friday the 13th.

By the 1950s, the original Thirteen Club was a distant memory.

A 1953 article in the *New York Times* about Friday the 13th confirms that the newspaper that had done so much to promote Captain Fowler's club no longer remembered its existence. London's Thirteen Club is mentioned, as is the short-lived National Society of Thirteen Against Superstition, Prejudice and Fear (more on that later), but the original Thirteen Club is overlooked.

Today, there are still a few active 13-related social clubs whose antics are occasionally covered by the media. Reflecting the popularity of the Friday the 13th superstition, they call themselves Friday the 13th clubs, and meet only on that date. The most notorious of these is a Friday the 13th club in Philadelphia, which is rumored to have disbanded at the start of the new millennium. In the main, these clubs have been inspired by postmortem newspaper accounts of the original Thirteen Club, or the London Thirteen Club. But they do not take the cause as seriously or show as much wit or originality in their approach. The Philadelphia club has deeper roots than most, dating back to the 1930s. It was likely a descendant of—or at least inspired by—the Philadelphia branch of the original New York Thirteen Club. Certainly the similarity of its rituals—sitting 13 to a table, walking under ladders, breaking mirrors, opening umbrellas indoors, and spilling salt on the table—rules out coincidence. However, in the 1990s, active members were unaware of the original Thirteen Club, and believed theirs to be the first of its kind.

Another contemporary phenomenon that appears to have been inspired by articles on the Thirteen Club is the Friday the 13th party. These, too, tend to resurrect the props and rituals of the Thirteen Club. In at least one case, the link is clear. In 1987, the *New York Times* ran a story in a short-lived social column called "The Evening Hours" about a Friday the 13th party attended by the rich and famous. The description of the party read like a carbon copy of an original Thirteen Club dinner; however, no mention was made of the club or its history. I couldn't help wondering if the story's appearance in the *New York Times*—the paper that had so often reported on the Thirteen Club—was coincidental. It turned out to be anything but. Searching for a good Friday the 13th story for the column, a *Times* reporter had stumbled upon an article about the original Thirteen Club in the paper's archives. When she called one of her sources—a publicist with a bevy of well-heeled clients—to ask her if the club might still be in existence, the publicist offered to throw a Friday the 13th party of her own, complete with broken mirrors, black cat silhouettes, spilled salt, etc. The arrangement worked out well: the publicist got her clients exposure in the paper, and the reporter got her story.

Outside of a few scattered references in print, the Thirteen Club has been completely forgotten, its legacy lost. The Thirteen Club and its intrepid members deserve to be remembered. It is hard to fathom today, but it took courage to reject a belief that had conquered the minds of so many. During its run of more than three decades, the Thirteen Club did its best to kill off the 13-at-a-table superstition; it *did* disprove it—thousands upon thousands of members sat 13 to a table and survived—but disproving and disbelieving are very different things. Despite the sustained, coordinated, and well-publicized efforts of some of the most influential people of the day, unlucky 13 at a table remained popular well into the twentieth century—but it did not outlive it. *The Amy Vanderbilt Complete Book of Etiquette*, a standard reference on social mores for today's "Evening Hours" crowd, observes: "It was once considered bad luck to have thirteen people at the dinner table, but no one pays attention to this superstition any longer." Like the Thirteen Club, the 13-at-a-table superstition is all but forgotten today.

CHAPTER TWO

The Origins of Unlucky 13

Many people believe that the superstition about sitting thirteen at tables dates from the Last Supper and the crucifixion of Jesus Christ. That is not possible, for the idea goes back centuries earlier; but it does seem clear that this world fatality gave the idea new life and sent it bounding forward along the years to come.

—Charles Platt, *Popular Superstitions* (1925)

I HAVE A CONFESSION to make: To me, 13 has always been just a number. I have never believed that 13 is unlucky or been tempted to thumb my nose at fate and make it my lucky number (I don't have one). I am neither a triskaidekaphobe nor a triskaidekaphile; in fact, before my visit to that roadside antique shop in Maine I didn't even know that fear of 13 is known as *triskaidekaphobia* or that its opposite, the belief that 13 is lucky, is called *triskaidekaphilia*. I was surprised to discover that the 13 superstition had inspired the creation of a social club aimed at its destruction, and not just any club—a club that counted among its members a powerful array of politicians, lawyers, journalists, and businessmen. I found myself wondering where unlucky 13 came from. *Miscellany* contained no information on 13 other than the articles on the Thirteen Club.

When I began to research the subject, I quickly discovered that over the past 150 years there has been a major shift in how people view the origins of unlucky 13. In the nineteenth century, there was a consensus that 13 at a table was the first 13 superstition and that it was inspired by the Last Supper. Today there is no consensus on either count. Some sources credit 13 at a table as the first unlucky 13, while others favor Friday the 13th. Contemporary newspapers and books usually follow the same formula when discussing unlucky 13's origin: They list several competing theories, then suggest that the 13 superstition is so ancient and its history so fragmentary that no one will ever know the truth. Many reject the Last Supper theory on the grounds that unlucky 13 predates the Christian era.

Although this revisionist trend did not become widespread until the twentieth century, the seeds were sown earlier. In the nineteenth century, every triskaidekaphobe *knew* that unlucky 13 originated with 13 at a table, and that 13 at a table was inspired by the Last Supper. The only people who questioned the Last Supper theory were skeptics who did not believe that 13 was unlucky and who, therefore, did not see any reason to trust the triskaidekaphobe's perspective on the origin of their beliefs. In the mid-nineteenth century, as triskaidekaphobia became more and more prevalent, skeptics began to speculate about alternative theories. By the late nineteenth and early twentieth centuries, the majority of books and articles on superstition (which tended to be written by nonbelievers) noted that most people *believed* that the origin of unlucky 13 was the Last Supper, but dismissed this as a reflection of the public's ignorance. Folklorists, authors, and journalists began to muddy the waters by searching for examples of unlucky 13 in cultures as diverse and far-removed from one another in time and geography as the Neanderthals, Ancient Egyptians, Babylonians, Ancient Greeks, Celts, Mayans, and Native Americans.

Over and over again, the same assumptions were made: if a culture in the past viewed some incarnation of 13 as unlucky or, more often, merely significant, then: (1) The belief in unlucky 13 must have been continuous all the years in between; and (2) Our belief must be derived from their belief. However, continuity of belief needs to be proved, not assumed. This is all the more criti-cal in the case of number superstitions because numerology has been so widely practiced in so many cultures throughout history that it is difficult to find a number between 1 and 24 that has not been considered unlucky by more than one culture. To establish the original source of unlucky 13, it is necessary to demonstrate a continuous chain of belief through time and across cultures, from its initial appearance to its emergence as the world's most popular superstition in the nineteenth century.

In the twentieth century, the proliferation and growing pop-ularity of alternative theories continued to undermine the Last Supper theory. Eventually even triskaidekaphobes began to lose their grasp of the connection between unlucky 13 and the Last Supper. Today, triskaidekaphobes are just as confused about the origins of 13 as everyone else. Over the course of the past century there have been many different theories about the origin of unlucky 13. Most flatly contradict all available evidence. Nonetheless, these theories have permanently transformed our understanding of unlucky 13's history. They have also laid the foundation for an anti-unlucky-13 movement that continues to be a significant force in the decline of the 13 superstition today.

12 + 1

Thirteen has meant bad luck to many for thousands of years, probably because man learned to count on his fingers plus two feet. That gave a nice, manageable, readily divisible 12; beyond lay the dreadful unknown.

—"Take Any Number," *New York Times* (October 13, 1963)

One of the most popular 13 theories is mathematical in nature: because twelve has long been associated with completeness (twelve gods on Mount Olympus, twelve signs of the zodiac, twelve months in a year, twelve apostles), 12 + 1 became associated with "completeness plus one"—uncertainty, unpredictability. This begs the question: why has twelve long been associated with completeness? Here, a correlate to the theory comes to the rescue: Prehistoric man learned to count on his ten fingers, then added his feet to get to twelve. Twelve represented the upper limit of prehistoric man's counting system, and we retain the cultural imprint of this early limitation. Taking this view, the unlucky 13 of the Last Supper was simply a further reflection of this early belief.

The first record I was able to find of this theory was in a book called *Popular Superstitions*, by Englishman Charles Platt, published in 1925. After postulating that "primitive man" first learned to count to ten on his fingers, Platt rejected the idea that he "calculated Eleven and Twelve mentally. This was a stupendous advance, but probably he 'thought' of his two feet, the left foot for Eleven, the right for Twelve." Platt concluded that 13

> was not used as a number, but as a vague word meaning anything beyond Twelve. To the untutored savage, as to the animal mind to-day, anything unknown conveyed an immediate sense of danger. Thirteen was not really an unlucky number, but a fateful one—a number full of vague and unimaginable possibilities, and therefore a number to be avoided by any peace-loving man.

There is, of course, no way to verify how man first learned to count. However, when anthropologists discovered extant cultures in the late nineteenth and early twentieth centuries that still used body-counting systems, none employed the ten-finger–two-feet method, and none had any difficulty moving beyond twelve. According to *The Universal History of Numbers*, at the end of the nineteenth century the Torres Straits islanders had a body-counting system that allowed them to count to thirty-three: 13 was represented by the right thumb, and every toe was assigned a specific number, too. (This seems reasonable—if you can count fingers, you can, and probably would, count toes.) The Papuans and Elema peoples of New Guinea ignored the feet altogether, keeping their body-counting systems above the belt: for the former, 13 was the left eye; for the latter, it was the right chest. Thirteen was accorded no special significance in any of the body-counting systems surveyed. The hyperbole with which the author of *Popular Superstitions* concludes his analysis of the mathematical origins of unlucky 13—"Thirteen is . . . a Fateful number—one to be dreaded and avoided because no man could fathom its immense possibilities!"—seems to be pure fantasy. Nonetheless, the ten-finger–two-feet theory is repeated to this day in dozens of newspaper articles, encyclopedia entries, and Web sites on superstition.

THE DEATH OF BALDUR

Where did the superstition begin? The answer, if there is one, lies so far back in time no one knows. . . . Early Christians blamed the Last Supper, at which Judas was the 13th guest. But long before then, Norse mythology was telling of a banquet for a dozen gods that was crashed by an evil spirit, Loki, who killed one of the guests with a poisoned arrow and caused a celestial uproar.

—"13th Floor, Anyone?" *New York Times* (June 5, 1977)

Based on the frequency with which it appears in print, the most compelling evidence that unlucky 13 predates the Last Supper is the myth of the death of Baldur in Norse mythology. Baldur, the god of light, is the son of Frigga, the supreme goddess, and Odin, the god of wisdom, poetry, war, and agriculture. When Baldur has nightmares suggesting his life is in danger, his mother extracts a promise from all things, animate and inanimate, that they will do nothing to harm him. Baldur's invincibility provides a new form of entertainment in Valhalla, the home of Odin, in Asgard, the citadel of the gods. To pass the time, the other gods use Baldur as target practice, honing their war craft by attacking him with rocks, darts, swords, and battle-axes—to their endless amusement. Baldur is honored by the attention; after all, invincibility is every warrior's dream. Enter Loki, who always appears in the Norse myths as an agent of evil. Jealous of the attention being paid to Baldur by the other gods, Loki assumes the shape of a woman and tricks Frigga into confessing that the only thing she neglected to protect her son against was a small shrub of mistletoe—because she thought it could not possibly harm him. Loki promptly fashions a spear of mistletoe and returns to Valhalla, where he presents it to Baldur's brother, Hodur, the blind god of winter, whose infirmity had prevented him from joining in the fun of attacking Baldur. With Loki guiding his arm, Hodur throws the spear at Baldur and kills him.

Unlucky 13 enters the picture because there were twelve gods in Valhalla before Loki intruded, making him the 13th—or so the story goes. The earliest known reference linking the 13 superstition and the death of Baldur appears in one of the nineteenth century's greatest best-sellers, E. Cobham Brewer's *Dictionary of Phrase and Fable*, first published in 1870. Under the entry "Thirteen Unlucky," Brewer writes: "Sitting down thirteen at dinner, in old Norse mythology, was deemed unlucky, because at a banquet in the Valhalla, Loki once intruded, making thirteen guests, and Baldur was slain." Brewer continues: "The superstition was confirmed by the Last Supper of Christ and His twelve apostles, but the superstition itself is much anterior to Christianity." Brewer took the myth as proof that the 13 superstition predated the Last Supper. Ever since its initial publication, his *Dictionary of Phrase and Fable* has been a standard reference book; countless newspaper stories, some published as recently as 2004, have followed Brewer's lead, claiming that the Norse myth is proof that unlucky 13 predates the Last Supper. A number are considerably less cautious and claim that the myth is the original source of the 13 superstition.

There are two problems with using Baldur's death to argue that the 13 superstition predates the Last Supper. First, there is no way to know whether or not Norse mythology predates the New Testament. In making his claim, Brewer relied on the popular assumption that all myths originate in that murky period in the distant past before the birth of organized religion. However, the first record of Baldur's death appears in the *Prose Edda*, which was written in the thirteenth century C.E. by the Icelandic poet Snorri Sturluson, two centuries *after* the conversion of Iceland to Christianity. In fact, some scholars argue that the parallels between Norse mythology and the New Testament reflect the influence of Christianity on the Norse myths.

The second (and insurmountable) problem with this theory is that a close reading of the *Prose Edda* reveals that 13 gods, not twelve, were present when Loki appeared with his mistletoe—making him the unlucky *fourteenth* guest. There is no mention of numbers in the death of Baldur myth itself, but earlier in the *Prose Edda* we learn that twelve seats were built for the gods in Valhalla, plus a special "high-seat" for Odin—13 seats for 13 gods. There is nothing in the myth to suggest that anyone was absent when Loki arrived, so there is no reason to believe that there were not 13 gods present.

Professor John Lindow of the University of California, Berkeley, an expert on Norse mythology and the author of *Murder and Vengeance Among the Gods: Baldur in Scandinavian Mythology*, concurs: "There is no connection between the number 13 and Baldur's death. The number 13 does not have any special significance in Scandinavian mythology." Whether or not this misapprehension began with E. Cobham Brewer, the success of his *Dictionary of Phrase and Fable* has helped keep the false connection between Norse myth and unlucky 13 alive for more than a century.

THE COVEN

One of the core historical "facts" about 13 circulating in newspapers and over the Internet is that a coven—the congregation of witches on the Sabbath—always consists of 13 members. With the rise of Wicca and other neopagan movements in the second half of the twentieth century, the theory emerged that at some point in the past the fear and hatred of witches carried over to the witch's number, giving it its negative connotation. There is a historical connection between 13 and witchcraft, although its significance is ambiguous. Beginning in the late sixteenth century in England, there are a handful of references to covens of 13 in witch-trial confessions.

The link between 13 and witchcraft might have remained obscure were it not for the work of Margaret Murray, an English Egyptologist who turned her attention to the history of English witchcraft when World War I prevented her from traveling to Egypt. In her influential 1921 book, *The Witch Cult in Western Europe*, Murray introduced a radical and seductive reinterpretation of the history of witchcraft. Her innovation was to discount the fact that witch-trial confessions were secured under extreme duress and that the prosecution often fed the accused the answers it wanted to hear. Taking the confessions—including the references to covens of 13—at face value, Murray arrived at the conclusion that witchcraft persecution did not represent the irrational expression of mass hysteria or the political and religious oppression of the outsider; it was a systematic attempt to destroy an integrated, competing pagan religion. She was convinced that she had uncovered "the beliefs, organization, and ritual of a hitherto unrecognized cult . . . practiced by many classes of the community." This was not just any cult; this was "the ancient religion of Western Europe," still flourishing in the seventeenth century.

In the years following the publication of *The Witch Cult in Western Europe*, academic folklorists thoroughly discredited Margaret Murray's theory, proving that her work used limited evidence of questionable validity, creative mathematics, and selective reasoning to arrive at a predetermined conclusion. This didn't stop *The Witch Cult in Western Europe* from turning contemporary beliefs about the history of witchcraft on their ear. The book's success led to Murray being commissioned by the *Encyclopedia*

Britannica to write the Witchcraft entry for the 1929 edition.
Murray did not pass up the opportunity to present her ideas to a
broader audience:

> When examining the records of the mediaeval witches, we
> are dealing with the remnants of a pagan religion which
> survived, in England at least, till the 18th century, 1,200
> years after the introduction of Christianity.... There were
> in each district a band of such persons, in number 13, *i.e.*, a
> chief or "devil" and 12 members. This band was known as a
> "Coven."

This essay, reprinted in every edition of the *Encyclopedia
Britannica* until 1969, became the primary source for the often-
repeated assertion that a coven consisted of 13 witches.

Popularized by the *Encyclopedia Britannica*, Murray's work
became one of the key inspirations for Wicca and other neopagan
movements in the twentieth century. Her theory that paganism
had survived intact through the centuries was taken one step further by the eccentric English occultist Gerald B. Gardner.
Gardner claimed to have been taught the old pagan ways by a
member of the last surviving coven of the ancient witch cult.
Beginning with a novel, *High Magic's Aid*, published in 1949
under a pseudonym, and continuing in the 1950s with a number
of nonfiction books, including one with an introduction by
Murray, Gardner introduced the world to the tenets of the alleged
witch cult, and advocated for a renewal of the ancient religion.
The rest, as they say, is history.

Margaret Murray's work continues to be a source of embarrassment to academic folklorists today, not least of all because for a time she was president of the UK's Folklore Society and publisher of *Folklore*, the oldest academic journal in the field. A 1994 article in the journal entitled "Margaret Murray: Who Believed Her, and Why?" attempted to distance the journal and the discipline from her legacy by downplaying the society's support of her work and by laying the blame for her enduring popularity at the doorstep of the *Encyclopedia Britannica* and the "journalists, filmmakers, popular novelists and thriller writers" who used the encyclopedia as a primary resource. In the article's estimation, Murray's ideas were here to stay: "By now they are so entrenched in popular culture that they will probably never be uprooted."

This assessment seems warranted if one looks at today's popular reference works. *Webster's Third New International Dictionary*, for example, published in 2002, defines a coven as "a congregation or assembly of witches; *specif*: a band of 13 witches." The history of the connection between witches and 13 parallels the history of the falsification of the myth of Baldur in Cobham Brewer's *Dictionary of Phrase and Fable*: an errant theory popularized by an entry in a widely distributed book has led to near-universal acceptance of a dubious "fact."

THE NEOPAGAN MOON

> Friday. Day of the Goddess Freya, called unlucky by Christian monks, because everything associated with female divinity was so called. Friday the 13th was said to be especially unlucky because it combined the Goddess's sacred day with her sacred number, drawn from the 13 months of the pagan lunar year. (See *Menstrual Calendar*.)
>
> —Barbara G. Walker, *Woman's Encyclopedia of Myths and Secrets* (1983)

Neopaganism has drawn inspiration from another 13—the most famous recurring 13 in nature—which is technically not a 13 at all. The moon, which waxes and wanes 12.41 times per solar year, is believed to have played a significant role in many early cultures, including in their calendar systems, which often followed a 13-month lunar cycle. In some cultures, the moon was associated with women, menstruation, and fertility. Because of this feminine-lunar connection, many twentieth-century neopagans, especially those with an interest in feminism, made the case that unlucky 13 originated with the rise of Christianity. They argued that patriarchal Christianity created the 13 superstition—primarily through the story of the Last Supper—as a way of undermining feminine pagan belief systems. This theory depends upon, among other things, the assumption that the Church *has* historically portrayed 13 as an unlucky number. This, however, is not the case. The Church has never viewed or encouraged the public to view 13 as unlucky at any point in its history; in fact, the opposite is true.

THE KNIGHTS TEMPLAR

On Friday 13, 1307, all Templars residing in France were arrested.... By nightfall 15,000 men were in chains and Friday the 13th had won a unique place for itself in the popular imagination as the most unlucky and inauspicious date in the calendar.

—Graham Hancock, *The Sign and the Seal:*
The Quest for the Lost Ark of the Covenant (1992)

Another popular theory about the origin of unlucky 13 is that it began with the annihilation of the Knights Templar at the hands of King Philip IV of France and Pope Clement V in the early fourteenth century. The Knights Templar was a monastic military order founded in Jerusalem in 1118 C.E., whose mission was to protect Christian pilgrims during the Crusades. Over the next two centuries, the Knights Templar became extraordinarily powerful and wealthy. Threatened by that power and eager to acquire their wealth, King Philip secretly ordered the mass arrest of all the Knights Templar in France on Friday, October 13, 1307—Friday the 13th. In 1312 Pope Clement collaborated with King Philip by demanding the arrest of all the Knights throughout Europe. The charges were blasphemy and witchcraft. The Templars were accused of a wide range of crimes, including the renunciation of Christ, celebrating the witches' Sabbath, homosexual acts, devil worship, and infanticide. Given the nature of the accusations and the authority of the accusers, the terrible punishment meted out to them is not a surprise. On a single day, fifty-nine Templars were burned alive in a field outside Paris. The torture and executions continued month after month. In 1314, the Knights Templar officially came to an end when its grand master, Jacques de Molay, was burned alive. Ever since, the theory goes, Friday the 13th has been unlucky.

The Knights Templar theory is unusual because it presupposes that Friday the 13th was the first 13 superstition. However, contrary to popular opinion, there is no historical evidence that the Friday the 13th superstition predates the twentieth century. According to Oxford University Press's *Dictionary of Superstitions*, the first known reference to Friday the 13th was in 1913, seven centuries after the demise of the Knights Templar.

CHAPTER THREE

The Rise of 13

Things, composed of such flimsy Materials as the Fancies
of a Multitude, do not seem calculated for a long Duration;
yet have these survived Shocks, by which even Empires
have been overthrown. . . .

—John Brand, *Observations on Popular Antiquities* (1777)

T HE TWO MAIN contenders for the original 13 superstition,
other than 13 at a table, are the general belief that 13 is an
unlucky number and the belief that Friday the 13th is an unlucky
day. Friday the 13th, the most popular 13 superstition today, is part
of an established Western tradition of lucky and unlucky days.
One of the earliest texts to document belief in lucky and unlucky
days is *Work and Days*, an 828-line poem by an Ancient Greek
farmer named Hesiod, which dates from around 700 B.C.E.
Completed just twenty years after Homer's *Odyssey*, *Work and
Days* is an invaluable guide to daily life in early Classical Greece.

Inspired by Hesiod's frustration with his brother Perses's inability to stay out of debt (and an unspecified legal wrangle between the two), *Work and Days* is pedantic, prosaic, and self-aggrandizing. Hesiod evidently hoped that by sharing with his brother the secrets of his own success, he would prevent his brother from shaming him further in the public eye. Not much is known about Hesiod's life beyond what he reveals in *Work and Days*—except that he was murdered. After reading his poem (in which he details his brother's many failings, including his propensity for violence), it is tempting to speculate that he may have been a victim of fratricide. Irrespective of its literary merits, *Work and Days* offers the contemporary reader unique insights into Ancient Greek culture—especially farming, navigation, and the influence of the calendar on peoples' decisions—which has made it a perennial favorite with classicists and historians.

An Ancient Greek in the eighth century B.C.E. believed that the lives of the gods held the key to which days were lucky or unlucky. It was possible to unravel the calendar's secrets by paying heed to what had befallen the gods on a given day. Thirteen figures in *Work and Days* only once. In a section of the poem containing advice on husbandry, Hesiod writes: "Avoid the thirteenth of the waxing month for beginning to sow: yet it is the best day for setting plants." To the Ancient Greek, the 13th day of the month was less auspicious than the first, fourth, and seventh (holy), the eighth and ninth (good for the works of man), and the eleventh and twelfth (excellent for shearing sheep and harvesting fruits). But the 13th fared better than the sixth (bad for planting and the birth of girls) and the fifth ("Avoid fifth days: they are unkindly and terrible"). According to Hesiod, both lucky and unlucky days were "a great blessing to men on earth" because they gave people some hold over fate, a way of garnering good fortune and avoiding bad. Much worse than even the most unkindly and terrible day of the month were the days about which nothing could be gleaned, since they were "changeable, luckless, and bring nothing." From this perspective, the ardent triskaidekaphobe is much better off than the skeptic who insists that days are luckless, because it is a blessing to know what to avoid in a changeable and unpredictable world.

With respect to 13, the list in *Work and Days* is typical of other lists of lucky and unlucky days over the centuries. When 13 is included, it isn't accorded any special consideration; there are always other dates that are equally or more unlucky; and no special significance is ever attributed to Friday the 13th. Some lists omit 13 entirely. In 1565, Richard Grafton, printer to King Edward VI, included the following list of "unlucky" and "very unlucky" days in his influential *Manuell of the Chronicles of England*:

The unlucky Days according to the opinion of the Astronomers are noted, which I have extracted as follows:—"January 1, 2, 4, 5, 10, 15, 17, 29, very unlucky. February 26, 27, 28, unlucky; 8, 10, 17, very unlucky. March 16, 17, 20, very unlucky. April 7, 8, 10, 20, unlucky; 16, 21, very unlucky. May 3, 6, unlucky; 7, 15, 20, very unlucky. June 10, 22, unlucky; 4, 8, very unlucky. July 15, 21, very unlucky. August 1, 29, 30, unlucky; 19, 20, very unlucky. September 3, 4, 21, 23, unlucky; 6, 7, very unlucky. October 4, 16, 24, unlucky; 6 very unlucky. November 5, 6, 29, 30, unlucky; 15, 20, very unlucky. December, 15, 22, unlucky; 6, 7, 9, very unlucky."

Of the sixty days of the year singled out as malevolent, not one was the 13th day of the month.

In 1696, another famous compendium on superstition and folklore was published in England—antiquarian John Aubrey's *Miscellanies Upon Various Subjects*. Aubrey also turned his attention to the popular subject of "day fatality, or some observations of days lucky and unlucky." Drawing on his vast personal library, he listed days that different cultures throughout history had viewed as significant, and then narrowed his focus to "more particular instances of lucky and unlucky days." True to his background as a miscellaneous writer—an authorial tradition in which books covered a wide variety of subjects, motivated less by argument or theme than by the author's range of interests—Aubrey's ruminations included examples from the lives of Alexander the Great, the duke of Lunenburg, Pope Sixtus V, his own maternal uncle, and himself. Thirteen was accorded no special significance in Aubrey's *Miscellanies*, except for the following, which appeared in a long list of historical notations:

The Romans counted Feb. 13, an unlucky day, and therefore they never attempted any business of importance; for on that day they were overthrown at Allia by the Gauls; and the Fabii attacking the city of the Veii, were all slain, save one.

At first glance, this might suggest a pre-Christian candidate in the lineage of unlucky 13. However, the Roman tradition of commemorating military defeats and national disasters as *dies atri*—"black days"—was followed so scrupulously that February 13th was only one of fifty-one days during the year when it was considered unlucky to undertake important business. There are no other references to an unlucky 13th day in Aubrey's work.

In lists of lucky and unlucky days prior to the nineteenth century, there is no pattern of Friday the 13th or the 13th day of the month being viewed as significant. In fact, I was unable to turn up a single nineteeth-century reference to Friday the 13th, which is consistent with the idea that the superstition did not emerge until the twentieth century. As for the general belief that 13 was an unlucky number, an extensive search of Western writing turned up no consistent references to unlucky 13 prior to the seventeenth century, when the earliest references to 13 at a table appear. Even in books about superstition, 13 is conspicuously absent. Reginald Scot's *The Discoverie of Witchcraft* (1584), for example, lists more than thirty contemporary superstitions of the "common peoples," including familiar superstitions like spilling salt, putting a shirt on inside out, stumbling, and a cat crossing one's path. Yet there is no mention of 13 being unlucky. What significant references there are before then to 13—e.g., the 13th man in *Beowulf* and the 13 seats Merlin constructed for King Arthur's Round Table—do not constitute superstitions, and, furthermore, seem, like 13 at a table, to be evocations of the Last Supper.

There is, however, one possible precursor to unlucky 13 at a table that does not have any obvious connection to the Last

Supper: Since its invention in Italy in the fifteenth century, the Death card in Tarot has consistently been the 13 card. According to Sir Michael Dummett, one of the preeminent philosophers of the twentieth century and an authority on the history of Tarot, the association of 13 with Death "occurs more frequently than the association of a particular number with any other card. . . . It is difficult to avoid the conclusion that the cardmakers, or those for whose taste they were catering, regarded this association as particularly appropriate, and strove to arrange it." This implies that there may have been a symbolic link between 13 and death in fifteenth-century Italy (which may or may not have also been inspired by the events of the Last Supper). However, an association is not the same thing as a superstition, and in the absence of any evidence that an unlucky 13 superstition existed in Western Europe prior to the seventeenth century, independent of its association with the Last Supper, it is safe to conclude that 13 at a table was the original 13 superstition.

13 AT A TABLE EMERGES

According to Oxford University Press's *Dictionary of English Folklore*, the first known reference to the 13 superstition is an allusion to unlucky 13 at a table that appeared in the English periodical *The Athenian Mercury* in June 1695. The reference in question, a ghost story, has survived because of antiquarian John Aubrey, who discovered it too late to include it in the first edition of his *Miscellanies*. The story finally made it into the 1857 edition. Part ghost story, part morality tale, it involves two ladies "of quality" who are close friends. When one falls ill with smallpox, the other refuses to visit because she is afraid of becoming infected. After her friend's death, she is visited by a stranger wearing a widow's dress and veil. She sends her servant down to see what the stranger wants, but is told that the message cannot be imparted to anyone but her. When she appears, the stranger lifts her veil, revealing herself to be the pox-ridden ghost of her close friend. Her message is a somber prophecy:

> You know very well, that you and I, loved entirely; and your not coming to see me, I took it so ill at your hands, that I could not rest till I had seen you, and now I am come to tell you, that you have not long to live, therefore prepare to die; and when you are at a feast, and make the thirteenth person in number, then remember my words.

After delivering its message, the ghost disappears, and the narrative picks up the woman's story at the crucial juncture: "To conclude, she was at a feast, where she made the thirteenth person in number." After the feast, her friend's brother asks her if it is true that his sister's ghost appeared before her—the story having apparently made the rounds. She says nothing in reply and begins to weep. Not long after, the ghost's prophecy comes true, and she dies.

If this were the only evidence that the 13-at-a-table superstition existed in the seventeenth century, the inference would be speculative at best. In the story, there is no suggestion that the protagonist will die within a year; the narrator does not imply that she died because she was one of 13 at a table; nor can one infer that there was a general belief at the time that to be one of 13 at a table had fatal consequences. Presumably, the protagonist herself did not believe that her death, prophesied by the ghost, would be triggered by being one of 13 at a feast, because unlike in nineteenth-century accounts of 13 at a table, she didn't express any trepidation at being one of 13. If the "thirteenth guest" element of the story was intended to have symbolic significance, it was probably an invocation of Judas and his betrayal of Jesus. By remembering the prophecy when she is one of 13 at a feast, the protagonist is invited to associate her own betrayal with Judas's. If her death was caused by anything, it was by her betrayal of that friendship. As a contemporary of the author's and an authority on topical popular beliefs, Aubrey was in a privileged position to assess the significance of *The Athenian Mercury* story. Referring to it as "a very pretty remark . . . concerning Apparitions" in his notes, he makes no mention of unlucky 13.

There are, however, two unequivocal seventeenth-century references to 13 at a table, both of which predate the *Athenian Mercury* story. The earliest reference appears in the memoirs of John Wilmot, second earl of Rochester, which were dictated on his deathbed in 1680 and published posthumously the following year. An infamous libertine and talented satirical poet who died at the age of thirty-three, Wilmot rediscovered religion near the end of his life. He was very interested in the phenomenon of people predicting their own deaths, which he interpreted as evidence that the soul was capable of divination. In his memoirs, he described the case of a chaplain who was a guest at his mother-in-law Lady Warre's house:

The Chaplain had dream't that such a day he should die, but being by all the Family put out of the belief of it, he had almost forgot it: till the Evening before at Supper, there being Thirteen at Table; according to a fond conceit that one of these must soon die, One of the young Ladies pointed to him, that he was to die. He remembring his Dream fell into some disorder, and the Lady Warre reproving him for his Superstition, he said, He was confident he was to die before Morning, but he being in perfect health, it was not much minded. It was Saturday-Night, and he was to Preach next day. He went to his Chamber and sate up late, as appeared by the burning of his Candle, and he had been preparing his Notes for his Sermon, but was found dead in his Bed the next Morning....

The second seventeenth-century reference to unlucky 13 at a table is found in an obscure book entitled *Of the Laws of Chance*, published in 1692. The author was John Arbuthnot, an early English statistician who is sometimes referred to as the father of statistics. The reference appears in a passage that offers gambling odds on, among other things, whether a pregnant woman will give birth to a boy or girl, whether "a *Woman* of Twenty Years old has her *Maidenhead*," and how large a group of people will yield an even chance that one will die within a year:

The Yearly Bills of Mortality are observ'd to bear such Proportion to the live People as 1 to 30, or 26; therefore it is an even Wager, that one out of thirteen, dyes within a Year (which may be a good reason, tho not the true one of that foolish piece of Superstition), because, at this rate, if 1 out of 26 dyes, you are no loser.

The London Bills of Mortality were a weekly listing of burials, which helped warn the city and public about the onset and progress of bubonic plague. Originating in the early sixteenth century, the bills gradually expanded to include information such as cause of death and age of the deceased, and became a key resource for statisticians.

If the "fond conceit" of unlucky 13 at a table emerged sometime in the late seventeenth century, and began in England, one does not have to look far to find a possible catalyst. In 1665, London was devastated by the Great Plague, which killed 70,000 people out of a population of 460,000. The London Bills of Mortality recorded its terrible progress, week after week. Books published in London that year were filled with desperate remedies and hysterical warnings and admonitions. Two representative titles: *A discourse of the plague containing the nature, causes, signs, and presages of the pestilence in general, together with the state of the present contagion: also most rational preservatives for families, and choice curative medicines both for rich and poor, with several waies for purifying the air in houses, streets, etc.*, and *The plague of the heart: its nature and quality, original and causes, signs and symptoms, prevention and cure: with directions for our behaviour under the present judgement and plague of the Almighty*. Many of the remedies and preventive measures contained in these books would have qualified as new superstitions had they outlasted the panic of the day. Because superstitions feed on uncertainty and fear, times of crisis increase the public's reliance on omens and augurs.

In 1665, the plague was seen as a sign of God's wrath—an ideal context for a reinterpretation of orthodox religious beliefs and conventions, and for the kind of magical thinking that gives rise to superstitions. Thanks to the Bills of Mortality, during this time numbers and probability began to play a larger role in prognostication than they ever had before. According to Arbuthnot, the mortality rates revealed in the London Bills of Mortality were not the source of the unlucky 13-at-a-table superstition. However, they did popularize the statistical relationship between population and death that is implicit in the superstition that if 13 people sit a table, one will die within a year.

In the early eighteenth century, unlucky 13 made another appearance in an English periodical. In 1711, the short-lived but influential *Spectator* published an anecdote about a gathering of 13 people, several of whom experienced "a panic terror" when they discovered their number—until someone pointed out that a woman in their party was pregnant, bringing the total number to 14. Even in the early days, unlucky 13 was considered a suitable subject for levity; the *Spectator* noted wryly that instead of the discovery portending death, "it plainly foretold one of them should be born." While there are a handful of other references to 13 at a table in the eighteenth century, the superstition was still a long way from its peak.

13 AND THE UNITED STATES

There is no evidence that unlucky 13 reached the United States before the nineteenth century. In fact, one of the principal arguments skeptics in the United States use to prove triskaidekaphobes wrong is the prominent, benevolent role 13 has played in the nation's history. It is true that the full title of the Declaration of Independence is The Declaration of Independence of the Thirteen Colonies, and that for the first fifteen years of its existence, the United States was the "thirteen united States of America." In the late eighteenth century, the number 13 symbolized the new nation's independence and unity. Every Fourth of July there was a 13-gun salute in honor of the 13 states. The 13-gun salute was a standard feature at the signing of treaties in the 1770s and 1780s. When George Washington's birthday began to be celebrated around the country in the 1780s, it, too, was accompanied by a 13-gun salute. Nor was 13 celebrated with ammunition alone. Thirteen toasts were offered at Fourth of July celebrations in acknowledgment of the 13 states. The 13-toast tradition ended abruptly in 1791, when Vermont became the 14th state; 13 toasts became 14. When Kentucky became the 15th state the following year, 14 became 15. Eventually, practical considerations (how many toasts can be made at a single event?) led to the tradition being abandoned. The 13-gun salute was also lost to history as new states were added. In 1841, the U.S. Navy finally fixed the number at 21, giving us a tradition that survives to this day.

Thirteen remained a benevolent number and a positive symbol of the birth of the nation beyond 1791—but not for very long.

The nineteenth century brought with it a strange new idea—one that in the span of a few decades would become the most popular and widespread superstition in the world. The number 13 was not a benevolent symbol of the U.S.'s independence; it was unlucky, and not just unlucky—mortally unlucky. Thirteen's sudden reversal of fortune in the United States is proof that cultural beliefs do not always evolve slowly, directed by significant historical forces; often, they can and do turn on a dime.

THE EMERGENCE OF THE OTHER UNLUCKY 13s

In the eighteenth century, the only references to unlucky 13 were to 13 at a table; 13 at a table *was* unlucky 13. Early in the nineteenth century, however, 13 at a table's growing popularity gave rise to the general number superstition and its many permutations. Scottish newspaperman and author Charles Mackay's 1841 book, *Extraordinary Popular Delusions and the Madness of Crowds*, captured the 13 superstition in the period of transition between 13 at a table and unlucky 13. In a section bemoaning the prevalence of superstitions that "alarm the vulgar and the weak," Mackay singled out 13 at a table for special condemnation: "If thirteen persons sit at a table, one of them will die within a year; and all of them will be unhappy. Of all evil omens this is the worst." In his assessment, "the great majority of people" subscribed to the superstition. Surveying the status of 13 in Europe, he distinguished between countries that still viewed 13 at a table as the only unlucky 13, and countries in which the "evil omen" of 13 at a table had begun to influence how people viewed 13 overall: "In almost every country of Europe the same superstition prevails, and some carry it so far as to look upon the number thirteen as in every way ominous of evil; and if they find thirteen coins in their purse, cast away the odd one like a polluted thing."

By the mid-nineteenth century, most of the familiar variations of unlucky 13 had made an appearance in Europe and the United States. In 1843, *Blackwood's Edinburgh Magazine* ran a story called "The Thirteenth: A Tale of Doom," which attested in dramatic fashion to the ill luck of being the 13th child born into a family. In 1850, Charles Dickens alluded to the superstition that a clock striking 13 portends a death in the family in his story, "A Christmas Tree." By this time the clock-striking-13 superstition was so pronounced that the English periodical *Notes and Queries: A Medium of Inter-Communication for Literary Men, Artists, Antiquaries, Genealogists* published extended correspondence from readers debating the veracity of a minor event that had occurred almost a century before: a soldier named James Hatfield, who had been accused of falling asleep on his watch, proved that he had been awake by testifying that the clock at St. Paul's Cathedral had struck 13 instead of 12 at midnight; others had also heard the aberration, and Hatfield was not court-martialed.

In 1858 in France, carriages and houses numbered 13 were considered unlucky. In the 1860s, P. T. Barnum wrote about unlucky Room 13 in his autobiography. Newspapers on both sides of the Atlantic highlighted occurrences of 13 in disasters at sea: launches on the 13th, accidents taking place on the 13th or involving a crew of 13. Thirteen had become the "sailorman's unlucky number." The 13th day of the month was increasingly considered unlucky. Parents began to make sure the name they chose for their children did not combine with the surname to make 13 letters. Two of today's most prominent 13 superstitions, however, had not yet made an appearance: the unlucky 13th floor, which was awaiting the innovation of the skyscraper, and unlucky Friday the 13th.

The history of the expression "baker's dozen," a popular colloquialism meaning 13, highlights a problem that can attend the emergence of a new superstition. In the mid-nineteenth century, caught up in the explosion of unlucky 13s, people no longer knew what to make of "baker's dozen." The tradition of the baker adding a 13th roll whenever a customer purchased a dozen was well established, but the public suddenly began to wonder if the tradition was related in some way to unlucky 13. Readers of *Notes and Queries*, a periodical that specialized in publishing and answering readers' queries on esoteric subjects, submitted letter after letter arguing both sides of the issue. What makes this interesting is that definitive proof that the baker's dozen had nothing to do with unlucky 13 was available to living memory. In the early part of the nineteenth century, a customer who bought a dozen rolls would receive one extra large roll or two extra small rolls, depending on the size rolls they were ordering. Originally, a baker's dozen was 13 *or* 14 rolls. This is why *Grose's Dictionary of the Vulgar Tongue* (subtitle: A Dictionary of Buckish Slang, University Wit, And Pickpocket Eloquence), published in 1810, defined a baker's dozen as "Fourteen; that number of rolls being allowed to the purchasers of a dozen."

This did not stop nineteenth-century revisionists from trying to bring "baker's dozen" under the expanding influence of unlucky 13. An anonymous 1880 story in *Harper's Monthly Magazine*, for example, claimed that the expression originated in 1655, when a witch demanded a 13th cookie for her dozen and the baker refused—until she put a curse on him. She removed the curse only after he promised that from then on, bakers would always add a 13th cookie to the dozen. This bit of whimsy may be the source of the twentieth-century belief that the 13th roll in a baker's dozen is payment to the devil to ward off bad luck. Although it has nothing to do with the superstition, today the baker's dozen is one of the familiar "facts" about unlucky 13 that encyclopedias and newspaper articles can be counted on to mention, even if the authors are a little vague about its precise significance.

In the late nineteenth century, the popularity of 13 superstitions attained new heights. Authors as diverse as Wilkie Collins, Fyodor Dostoevsky, Henrik Ibsen, Leo Tolstoy, Jules Verne, and Oscar Wilde invoked unlucky 13 in their work. Not coincidentally, this was also the period that spawned the Thirteen Club, the first coordinated attack on the superstition. Despite the proliferation of unlucky 13 superstitions, until the ascendance of Friday the 13th in the second decade of the twentieth century, no variation of unlucky 13 threatened the original—13 at a table—as the most popular. However, there was a subtle shift in the public's conception of 13 away from 13 at a table, which made possible the proliferation of alternative theories about the origin of 13. In the late nineteenth century, more and more people viewed 13 as generally unlucky, and unlucky 13 at a table as merely a prominent example of that superstition—instead of its progenitor.

THE TWENTIETH CENTURY

At the turn of the century, unlucky 13 was still the only superstition to merit its own headlines, year after year, in U.S. papers. In 1896, the *New York Times* tried to answer once and for all "Is Thirteen Unlucky?" They surveyed "a large number of railroad, army, navy, police, and fire department authorities"—the institutions most vulnerable to the vagaries of chance—and concluded: "Thirteen seems about as good as any other number." In the process of arriving at that hopeful conclusion, the article unwittingly revealed how pervasive the superstition was among "men of affairs." In general, railroads did not omit 13 from their trains the way airlines would later—but the superstition was popular among rail travelers and employees alike. It was common knowledge that tickets for berth 13 were the hardest to sell on a train. One railroad official confessed, "Locomotive engineers as a class are superstitious with reference to No. 13." It was not unheard of for an engine to be renumbered if it seemed particularly unlucky; one respondent recalled that Engine 1313 on a Pennsylvania line was renumbered after it got into two wrecks and engineers refused to man it.

The article revealed that wherever there was a 13, there was sure to be talk of bad luck. A number of fire departments observed that bad luck seemed to dog whoever wore badge number 13. "Chief Engineer Guthrie of Sacramento finds from his records that badge No. 13 is apparently a hoodoo, with a record of suspension, illness, and, in one case, a fatal shooting, for those who wore it." A similar history with badge number 13 in Detroit led new members of the company to avoid it: "One or two officers have paled when presented with the badge, and on one or two occasions it has been exchanged for another at the request of the recipient." Some fire departments reported bad luck with alarm box number 13 in their city—more fires in that district, more accidents and fatalities when its alarm was answered. Others recalled more large fires on the 13th of the month than chance would seem to dictate. Nor were street addresses exempt: according to the fire department in Bay City, Michigan, the house at Thirteenth and Frazer Streets in that city had "been a source of trouble to the department for the last eighteen years, no matter who lived there."

Things were no different in police departments across the country. In Springfield, Illinois, the department removed badge 13 from commission. In Poughkeepsie, New York, the police chief allowed the policeman wearing badge 13 to reverse the numbers and become number 31. Those who did not take such precautions apparently had occasion to regret it. In Sioux City, Iowa, the history of badge 13 was a litany of misfortune for six successive policemen:

1) Discharged for neglect of duty

2) Clubbed on election day

3) Dismissed for cause

4) Resigned because of ill fortune

5) Shot himself in the foot

6) Fell from a car

Three years after the *New York Times*'s investigation of 13, an Evanston, Illinois, policeman discovered that people's belief in unlucky 13 was enough to make wearing badge 13 unlucky.

Assigned the task of going door to door to warn local housewives to conserve water during a "water famine," he had so many doors slammed in his face that he returned to the police station and threatened to quit unless he was assigned a new number.

One of the earliest studies to assess the prevalence of superstitions in the United States was Fletcher Bascom Dresslar's *Superstition and Education*, published in 1907. Nearly two thousand college students were invited to write down on separate sheets of paper all the superstitions they knew. They were asked to indicate on each sheet whether they had "no belief," "partial belief," or "full belief" in the superstition. Dresslar's goal—to "peep into that darkly veiled but interesting mental realm which holds preserved remnants of our psychic evolution, as well as those ethnic impulses which are responsible for much of our present behavior"—was evidence of the social significance ascribed to superstition at the beginning of the twentieth century. The study revealed that "Thirteen is an unlucky number" was tied with "If you drop the dish rag, you will have company" as the most popular superstition. Of the 137 students who wrote down unlucky 13, 45 percent believed it "partially" or "fully." (Exactly 13 believed it fully!) Separate from "Thirteen is an unlucky number," 115 students wrote down the 13-at-a-table superstition, bringing 13's overall total to 252, with 48 percent of students stating that they believed the 13 superstitions "fully" or "partially." Since Dresslar did not separate out individual students, there is no way to know how many wrote down both 13 superstitions; however, it is all but certain that the total number of students who wrote down a 13 superstition exceeded the number who wrote down dropping-the-dish-rag—which would make unlucky 13 the best-known superstition of the day.

Part of what makes this study less rigorous than recent studies on superstition is also what makes it more interesting. Because subjects were allowed to write down the superstitions in their own words, rather than indicating their attitudes toward a prescribed list, the study captured two distinct strains of the 13-at-a-table superstition: 76 subjects favored "If thirteen sit together at a table, one of the number will die before the year ends," while 39 preferred the weaker version, "It is bad luck to sit at the table when thirteen are present." These are two very different superstitions, especially to a triskaidekaphobe who has the misfortune of being one of the 13 at a table. The triskaidekaphobe who believes in the fatal version is going to leave the table much more quickly and with less ceremony than the one who simply looks at it as bad luck.

The rise of 13 is not the story of one superstition, but of dozens, each with its own distinct variations—all of which can be traced back to the emergence of unlucky 13 at a table in the seventeenth century. As for the future of unlucky 13, of the nearly two thousand students who participated in the 1907 study, only two mentioned the date Friday the 13th. One partially believed and one didn't believe that "If the 13th day of the month comes on a Friday, evil things are more likely to happen than at any other time." In the first decade of the twentieth century, unlucky Friday the 13th—the 13 superstition that would eventually replace 13 at a table as the most popular superstition in the world—was still in its infancy.

LITERARY 13

1

There is no end to the old houses, with resounding galleries, and dismal state-bedchambers, and haunted wings shut up for many years, through which we may ramble, with an agreeable creeping up our back, and encounter any number of ghosts.... There is a haunted door, that never will keep open; or another door that never will keep shut, or a haunted sound of a spinning-wheel, or a hammer, or a footstep, or a cry, or a sigh, or a horse's tramp, or the rattling of a chain. Or else, there is a turret-clock, which, at the midnight hour, strikes thirteen when the head of the family is going to die.

—Charles Dickens, *A Christmas Tree* (1850)

2

He rushed to the door, listened, caught up his hat and began to descend his 13 steps cautiously, noiselessly, like a cat. He had still the most important thing to do—to steal the axe from the kitchen. That the deed must be done with an axe he had decided long ago.

—Fyodor Dostoevsky, *Crime and Punishment* (1866)

3

In the Levins' house, so long deserted, there were now so many people that almost all the rooms were occupied, and almost every day it happened that the old princess, sitting down to table, counted them all over, and put the thirteenth grandson or granddaughter at a separate table.

—Leo Tolstoy, *Anna Karenina* (1877)

4

"Superstitious, indeed! You don't know what my experience has been. My only sister was one of a party of thirteen at dinner; and she died within the year."

—Wilkie Collins, *I Say No* (1884)

5

"Thirteen! Ah, that is indeed a lucky number," replied the Tin Woodman. "All my good luck seems to happen on the thirteenth. I suppose most people never notice the good luck that comes to them with the number 13, and yet if the least bit of bad luck falls on that day, they blame it to the number, and not to the proper cause."

"Thirteen's my lucky number, too," remarked the Scarecrow.

"And mine," said Scraps. "I've just thirteen patches on my head."

—L. Frank Baum, *The Patchwork Girl of Oz* (1913)

6

Mr. Bloom stood far back, his hat in his hand, counting the bare heads. I'm thirteen. No. The chap in the macintosh is thirteen. Death's number. Where the deuce did he pop out of? He wasn't in the chapel, that I'll swear. Silly superstition that about thirteen.

—James Joyce, *Ulysses* (1922)

7

"You belong to a Thirteen Club," said the poet. "You walk under a ladder on Friday to dine thirteen at a table, everybody spilling the salt. But even you don't go into those trees at night."

—G. K. Chesterton, *The Trees of Pride* (1922)

8

One of my selves, the one which in the past had been in the habit of going to those barbarian festivals that we call dinner-parties, at which, for the men in white shirt-fronts and the half-naked women in feathered plumes, values have been so reversed that a man who does not turn up after having accepted the invitation—or merely arrives after the roast has been served—is deemed to have committed an act more culpable than any of those immoral actions which, along with the latest deaths, are so lightly discussed at this feast which nothing but death or a serious illness is an acceptable excuse for failing to attend—and then only provided that one has given notice in good time of one's intention to die, so that there may be no danger for the other guests of sitting down thirteen at a table—this one of my selves had retained its scruples and lost its memory.

—Marcel Proust,
Remembrance of Things Past: Time Regained (1927)

9

"It is unfortunate that they are as they are, but without them I could have never reached the perfection that I am sure we are to find here," and he tapped lovingly upon the heavy glass cover of the vat before which he stood. "And this is but the beginning. There can be no more mistakes now, though I doubt if we can ever improve upon that which is so rapidly developing here." Again he passed his long, slender hand caressingly over the coffin-like vat at the head of which was a placard bearing the words, Number Thirteen.

—Edgar Rice Burroughs, *The Monster Men* (1929)

10

It was a bright cold day in April, and the clocks were striking thirteen.

—George Orwell, *1984* (1949)

11

"At last," sighed Madeline, "we are able

To sit down without being thirteen at table."

—Ludwig Bemelmans, *Madeline in London* (1961)

12

Thirteenth floor. Research and Development. Hang about. Thirteenth floor....

He suddenly remembered the floor-display panel in the elevator. It hadn't had a thirteenth floor. He'd thought no more about it because, having spent fifteen years on the rather backward planet Earth, where they were superstitious about the number thirteen, he was used to being in buildings that numbered their floors without it. No reason for that here, though. The windows of the thirteenth floor, he could not help noticing as he flashed swiftly by them, were darkened.... What was going on behind the darkened windows of the sealed-off thirteenth floor?

—Douglas Adams, *Mostly Harmless* (1992)

13

We talked some about Indianapolis, which I had seen on the same trip, and where she and her husband had been a waitress and a bartender for a Thirteen Club—before they joined the army of the King of Michigan.

I asked her what the club was like on the inside.

"Oh, you know—" she said, "they had stuffed black cats and jack-o-lanterns, and aces of spades stuck to the tables with daggers and all. I used to wear net stockings and spike heels and a mask and all. All the waitresses and bartenders and the bouncer wore vampire fangs."

—Kurt Vonnegut, *Slapstick: Or Lonesome No More!* (1999)

CHAPTER FOUR

The Sin of 13

> It is difficult to mark the limits of superstition.... Who will judge this great matter? Will it be reason? But each sect claims to have reason on its side.
>
> —Voltaire, *Philosophical Dictionary* (1764)

IF 13 AT a table was the first 13 superstition, the obvious parallels between the superstition and the Last Supper make the latter a strong candidate for being the source of unlucky 13. Many of the alternative theories about the origin of unlucky 13 take a different view. They claim that unlucky 13 predates the Last Supper, and that the Last Supper merely helped to perpetuate the superstition. The only alternative theory that credits the Last Supper as the source—neopagan moon—argues that the treatment of 13 in the New Testament was a calculated attempt to undermine pagan religions that saw 13 as a benevolent number. One of the problems shared by these theories is their assumption that unlucky 13 has existed continuously in Western culture at least since the New Testament. Not only is there no evidence to support this, there is plenty of evidence that 13 was not considered unlucky in biblical times, and, moreover, that Christianity never encouraged the 13 superstition in the intervening centuries.

If repetition is a measure of numerological significance in the Bible, 13 was not an especially important number. It appears just fifteen times; *thirteenth* appears fourteen times. Compared to other numbers that are traditionally viewed as significant in Western culture—*twelve*, for instance, appears 212 times; *ten* 277 times; *seven* 515 times; *three* 570 times—13 slips into obscurity. None of the explicit references to 13 in the Bible ascribe any special significance to the number, certainly nothing that connects it to death, bad luck, or any of the associations we have today. There are, however, at least three implicitly negative 13s in the Bible. Two passages suggest a negative connotation for 13 by virtue of the role they assign to the number twelve. In the Gospel of John, there is a reference to the division of the day into twelve hours:

JOHN (11:9): Jesus answered, Are there not twelve hours in the day? If any man walk in the day, he stumbleth not, because he seeth the light of this world.
JOHN (11:10): But if a man walk in the night, he stumbleth, because there is no light in him.

According to this division of the day, the 13th hour would be the beginning of night—the time of uncertainty and danger when a man might be inclined to lose his footing. There is, incidentally, a long-standing superstition in many cultures that it is bad luck to stumbleth; even in Cicero's day it was a popular omen.

There is another 13-by-omission in the Apocrypha.

ESDRAS (14:10): For the world hath lost his youth, and the times begin to wax old.

ESDRAS (14:11): For the world is divided into twelve parts, and the ten parts of it are gone already. . . .

If the world were divided into twelve temporal phases, then the 13th phase would be the Apocalypse—the end of the world.

Although these references jibe with the idea that because 13 is one more than twelve it was considered "a number full of vague and unimaginable possibilities," all the explicit 13s scattered throughout the Bible are neutral or positive in their connotations. While twelve clearly had a positive connotation, there is no evidence that this had the effect of making 13 unlucky.

The third negative 13 in the Bible is certainly unlucky, but played no part in the emergence of the 13 superstition. In biblical times, flagellation was a customary punishment for crimes and transgressions; throughout the Old Testament there are many references to people being whipped or whipping others. The same is true of the New Testament: in the Gospel of Matthew, Christ predicted that he and his disciples would be whipped; in the Gospel of John, Christ himself used the "scourge" on the money changers. The law at the time stated that no more than forty stripes could be administered in punishment, so the custom developed of giving transgressors "forty stripes save one"—thirty-nine stripes across the back. Since whips consisted of three leather lashes, transgressors were whipped a total of 13 times.

THE LAST SUPPER

No one under the spell of the 13-at-a-table superstition in the nineteenth century blamed unlucky 13 on biblical whippings or the 13th hour of the day or the 13th phase of the world. Everyone knew that unlucky 13 owed its reputation to the events of the Last Supper. The most significant appearance of 13 in the Bible is as indirect as the others. Nowhere in the accounts of the betrayal of Christ in the Gospels of Matthew, Mark, Luke, or John does the number or word *thirteen* appear. The passage that is usually quoted as the source of unlucky 13 in the New Testament is a scene from the Gospel of John that does not even take place at the Last Supper:

> JOHN (6:70): Jesus answered them, Have not I chosen you twelve, and one of you is a devil?
> JOHN (6:71): He spake of Judas Iscariot [the son] of Simon: for he it was that should betray him, being one of the twelve.

The wording is interesting because it suggests that the significant grouping here is twelve, not 13; a devil is secreted among the twelve disciples of Christ, not—of course—among the twelve disciples *and* Christ. The other accounts of the betrayal and the

Last Supper in the New Testament support this interpretation. In all, the phrase "one of the twelve" is used seven times to refer to Judas as the betrayer of Christ. In the Gospel of Luke, there is this variation: "Then entered Satan into Judas surnamed Iscariot, being of the number of the twelve" (22:3). Nowhere in the New Testament is Judas, a devil, or Satan, and the number 13 linked; the numerological emphasis is always on *twelve*. This suggests that the authors of the New Testament never *intended* to convey the idea that 13 was unlucky.

There are other problems with using the Last Supper to argue that 13 was intended to be unlucky: The Last Supper was only one of any number of meals that Christ and his twelve disciples spent together. If the intention was to single out the grouping of 13 as unlucky, this would imply that their other meals together, including their sabbaths, were unlucky; and it would mark the ritual itself as unlucky. More to the point, it is inconceivable that the New Testament's authors would have wittingly embraced the blasphemy of implying that a group that included Jesus Christ—the son of God, the savior of man—was unlucky.

If there was any intended numerological significance to the Last Supper and the betrayal of Christ, the message cannot have been that 13 was unlucky. If, on the other hand, the significant number was supposed to have been twelve, this invites an interpretation that is at least consistent with the religious themes of the narrative. Perhaps it is not a coincidence that "one of the twelve" betrays Christ; twelve has a long history as a positive and benevolent number in mythology and folklore. That the number of the chosen from which the betrayer springs is benevolent twelve underscores the message that the devil can corrupt any of us, and that we must remain vigilant; no number of men is safe— no *number* is safe, not even twelve. Whether or not this was the authors' intention, the message is certainly more in line with biblical themes than the idea that 13 is unlucky.

CHRISTIANITY'S BENEVOLENT 13

Given the popularity of the neopagan moon and coven theories, it was a surprise to discover that the Church has always had a positive view of 13. From its earliest days, Christianity has considered 13 a benevolent number precisely *because* of its association with Christ and his twelve disciples. To the Christian, 13 represented the benevolent 13 of Christ and his disciples in general, not the fateful 13 of the Last Supper. In 426 C.E., St. Augustine, an avid numerologist, announced his successor as bishop before an assembly of his congregation and other clergy. In a letter describing the occasion, he wrote that those gathered called out 13 times, "O Christ, hear us; may Augustine live long!" Later on, during his farewell speech, they shouted 13 times, "To God be thanks! To Christ be praise!" Not only did his audience show no fear in repeating their invocation to Christ 13 times, but St. Augustine himself did not shy away from recording the precise number for posterity.

In emulation of Christ and his twelve disciples, St. Gregory the Great, pope from 590 to 604 C.E., initiated a tradition of hosting a dinner for twelve poor men (which, of course, placed him in the role of Christ). There was also a long tradition of new monasteries being founded by 13 monks: in 1031, the Abbey of Abdinghof began with 13 Benedictine monks; in 1132, 13 monks of the Cistercian order founded a monastery in York, England; in 1145, Pope Lucius II requested that Abbot Peter of Cluny send 13 monks to Rome to found the monastery St. Sabas on the Aventine; and so on.

The tradition of honoring Christ and his disciples by invoking 13 was not limited to monasteries; alms, endowments, and wills intentionally echoed this benevolent 13. John Stratford, archbishop of Canterbury during the fourteenth century, gave alms three times per day to 13 poor people. In the early sixteenth century, England's King Henry VII endowed Westminster Abbey with a pension for 13 poor men; his mother, Lady Margaret Beaufort, did the same for 13 poor women. Alexander Nowell, confessor to Queen Elizabeth I, donated two hundred pounds per year to maintain 13 scholars at Oxford University. Queen Elizabeth fulfilled the intentions of her late father, Henry VIII, by establishing a fund for 13 Alms-Knights (indigent veterans of English wars). Similar 13 traditions honoring Christ and his disciples existed throughout Europe.

Not every Christian invocation of 13 was as noble or altruistic. Bartolomé de Las Casas's fascinating 1552 indictment of the Indian genocide during Spain's conquest of the West Indies, *Brevísima relación de la destrucción de las Indias* (*A Short Account of the Destruction of the Indies*), included a description of a horrific invocation of the benevolent Christian 13, which took place on the island of Hispaniola (Dominican Republic):

They erected certain Gallowses, that were broad but so
low, that the tormented creatures might touch the ground
with their feet, upon every one of which they would hang
thirteen persons, blasphemously affirming that they did it
in honor of our Redeemer and his Apostles, and then putting fire under them, they burnt the poor wretches alive.

Another corruption of the Christian 13 may explain the
recurrence of references to covens of 13 in seventeenth-century
witch-trial confessions. Given the Church's association of 13 with
Christ and his disciples, accusing alleged witches of gathering in
covens of 13—"a chief or 'devil' and twelve members"—would
have been an accusation of blasphemy of the highest order. It may
be that the references to covens of 13 in witch-trial confessions,
which inspired Margaret Murray's witch cult theory, were reflections of the religious zeal and triskaidekaphilia of the accusers
rather than objective evidence of the existence of a witch cult that
embraced 13. In any case, it is clear that the neopagan moon theory, which presupposes that historically the Church has characterized 13 as unlucky, has no basis in fact.

SUPERSTITION DEFINED

Until the twentieth century, *superstition* was almost always
defined in opposition to religion—as an errant belief that contra-
dicted religious orthodoxy, or the beliefs of a competing religion.
The word is derived from the Latin *superstitio*, meaning "to stand
over or next to" in fear, wonder, or dread. In the last century

B.C.E., Cicero defined superstition as "the baseless fear of the gods, religion the pious worship." Thirteen centuries later, St. Thomas Aquinas defined it as "a vice contrary to religion by excess, not that it offers more to the divine worship than true religion, but because it offers divine worship either to whom it ought not, or in a manner it ought not." For Aquinas, superstition and atheism were the polar extremes of religious belief; equidistant between them was true religious faith.

This perspective on superstition survived into the twentieth century. *The Catholic Encyclopedia*, a Church-sanctioned 15-volume opus published between 1905 and 1915, expressed the relationship this way: "Superstition sins by excess of religion, and this differs from the vice of irreligion, which sins by defect." *The Catholic Encyclopedia* was the first encyclopedia of its kind, the Church's response to the growing popularity of general encyclopedias at the turn of the century.

In a further indication of the prevalence of unlucky 13 in the early twentieth century, the *Catholic Encyclopedia*'s entry for superstition singles out 13 as worthy of special condemnation: "The number thirteen continues to strike terror into the breasts of men who profess not to fear God." The *Encyclopedia* places fear of 13 in a relatively minor category of superstitions—"vain observances in daily life"—that stands apart from the "principle species of superstition—idolatry, divination, occult art"—with which the Church is most concerned. However, in the eyes of the Church,

Superstition of any description is a transgression of the First Commandment: "I am the Lord thy God—thou shalt not have strange gods before me. Thou shalt not make to thyself a graven thing, nor the likeness of anything that is in heaven above, or in the earth beneath ... thou shalt not adore them nor serve them" (Exod., xx, 2–5).... Such objective sinfulness is inherent in all superstitious practices from idolatry down to the vainest of vain observances, of course in very different degrees of gravity.

The belief that the events of the Last Supper marked 13 as an unlucky number and 13 at a table as mortally unlucky met the Catholic standard for a superstition: a vice contrary to religion by excess, offering divine worship in a matter in which it ought not. To a Catholic reader circa 1915, a book on unlucky 13 would have been a work of considerable moral and ethical import—a book on sin.

It is only in Christian religious writing that one will find the complaint that people are more frightened of unlucky 13 than of God. Judaism also has a long tradition of viewing 13 as a benevolent number. But in Judaism there has never been a split between the religious orthodoxy and practitioners on the significance of 13. The Jewish benevolent 13 tradition has remained intact for the past two hundred years, despite the explosion in popularity of the 13 superstition. What has inured it to triskaidekaphobia? The Jewish tradition has nothing to do with the Christian association of 13 with Christ and the disciples. If unlucky 13 originated as a reinterpretation of the significance of the Last Supper, one would expect the superstition to have little or no impact on the Jewish perspective on 13.

ANTIQUITATES VULGARE

A survey of pre-nineteenth-century Christian works aimed at eradicating superstition provides further evidence that unlucky 13 did not emerge as a prominent superstition before the early nineteenth century. In 1725, English curate Henry Bourne published *Antiquitates Vulgare* (*Antiquities of the Common People*), a progenitor of the modern discipline of folklore. Today, *Antiquitates Vulgare* is remembered as a unique compendium of the everyday beliefs, customs, and superstitions of early-eighteenth-century Britons—with speculation (of varying reliability) on their origins. In Bourne's day, however, *Antiquitates Vulgare* was a different kind of work entirely: a calculated, ambitious effort to destroy a force that in the author's view exercised more influence over "the ignorant Part of the World" than the "Word of GOD." Bourne announced his intentions on the title page:

An Account of Several of their
OPINIONS and CEREMONIES.
With
Proper REFLECTIONS upon each of them; showing
which may be retained, and which should be laid aside.

By tracing the origin of popular superstitions, Bourne was attempting to demystify and contextualize beliefs that the Church viewed as sinful, as a first step toward eradicating them. If he could show people where their superstitions came from and how they had evolved over time, he could undermine the mystical hold they had over them. Bourne attributed the superstitions of his day to two sources: "the Produce of Heathenism" and "the Invention of indolent Monks, who having nothing else to do, were the Forgers of many silly and wicked Opinions, to keep the World in Awe and Ignorance."

Bourne's book illustrates the challenges that an early-eighteenth-century Christian faced when trying to determine which popular customs and beliefs were superstitions. For Bourne, the final measure of the validity of any belief was its conformity with the Bible; over and over again, he analyzes popular beliefs by applying relevant passages from it. To him, the Bible was a collection of literal truths. And because he took the Bible literally—believing in a world filled with devils, angels, spirits, and countless miracles and omens—it was all the more difficult to distinguish between truth and superstition. Since much of *Antiquitates Vulgare* focused on omens, one of Bourne's challenges was to reconcile the many accepted (and glorified) omens in the Bible with the eighteenth-century Christian perspective that believing in omens was in and of itself a sin. His solution was to assume that not everything that was possible in biblical times was still possible in the eighteenth century.

> In these early Ages of the World, GOD permitted such Things upon extraordinary Occasions, to be asked by his own People. But they were only peculiar to those Times. We have no Warrant for doing the like.... The Observation of Omens, such as the falling of Salt ... are sinful and diabolical: They are the inventions of the Devil, to draw

men from a due Trust in God, and make them his own
Vassals.

Bourne was more tolerant of extrareligious customs and ceremonies than he was of omens. In the category of "harmless customs," he included several traditions we still observe—putting
flowers on graves, wishing people happy New Year—and others
that have been abandoned—the New Year's gift and "watching
with the dead" (the custom of staying with the deceased until
their body was carried to the grave). Conversely, Bourne admonished the public to abandon some traditions that are still with
us, including Christmas carols, Valentine's Day, and the fear of
walking through graveyards at night.

Nowhere in *Antiquitates Vulgare* does Bourne refer to 13 as a
contemporary superstition. The number appears only once, in a
chapter on superstitions about wells and fountains (a popular category of superstition at the time). In discussing the history of well
superstitions, Bourne describes *Fontinalia,* an ancient Roman
feast celebrated on October 13, which honored the nymphs that
were thought to reside in wells and fountains: believers decorated
wells with a crown of flowers and threw flowers into fountains.

In 1777, English antiquarian and curate John Brand published *Observations on the popular antiquities of Great Britain*, an
expanded, annotated version of Henry Bourne's *Antiquitates
Vulgare.* Brand's edition reproduced Bourne's work in its entirety,
but each chapter was followed by a chapter of commentary, much
of it unkind. Evidently, some of Bourne's conclusions seemed as
bizarre in 1777 as they do today. For example, Bourne hypothesized

that the once-widespread custom of setting bonfires on Mid-summer Eve was a relic of an earlier tradition of setting fire to wells, which he credited to a belief that dragons liked to "sperma-tize" wells; setting fire to the well water made it safe to drink. Brand implies that Bourne invented this theory out of whole cloth. What Brand does to Bourne is an author's worst night-mare: he not only openly derides his predecessor's work, he reproduces it in full and then puts a new title and name—his own—on the cover.

By 1777, the "English Antique" had become a fashionable subject of study. Brand's book was more widely distributed than Bourne's and quickly replaced it as the definitive work on English antiquities. Like Bourne, Brand saw superstition as the enemy of both God and man: "No Bondage seems so dreadful as that of Superstition: It hath ever imposed the most abject kind of Slavery." Writing a half-century later, Brand did not believe that everything in the Bible could be taken literally. This allowed him to apply a standard of credulity to which Bourne did not have access, and to make an assessment based on the *likelihood* of something being true. In this comprehen-sive, eclectic work, which ranges over a veritable menagerie of auguries—crows, ravens, owls, magpies, cocks, hens, crickets, spiders, maggots, hares, cats, weasels, and sheep—not to men-tion the superstitious implications of spittle and accumulations of dirt on gates and candle wicks, there is no mention of unlucky 13 or unlucky 13 at a table. Brand does, however, add a second 13th-day reference to the work, noting that December 13 was a fated day according to "the ancient Calendar of the

Church of Rome, 'That on this Day Prognostications of the Months were drawn for the whole Year.' "

John Brand died in 1806. In 1813, a posthumous edition of *Popular Antiquities* was published with additions drawn from manuscripts Brand left at the time of his death. By then, Henry Bourne's name had disappeared entirely from the book. Unlike previous editions, the 1813 edition contained a reference to unlucky 13: "The number thirteen is considered as extremely ominous, it being held that, when thirteen persons meet in a room, one of them will die within a year." As evidence, Brand quoted from a brief letter to the editor in the English periodical *The Gentleman's Magazine* in 1796. Signed *Incredulous*, the letter recounted how the conviviality of a recent dinner party "was suddenly interrupted by the discovery of a maiden lady, who observed that our party consisted of thirteen." After determining that no other guests were due to join them, "She was then fully assured that one of the party would die within the twelvemonth." *Incredulous* asked the editor if he or other readers could explain "the origin of this vulgar error." Two years later, in 1798, a reader named Camilla wrote to the magazine to explain that the superstition "may probably have arisen from the Paschal [Last] Supper. We none of us forget what succeeded that repast, and that thirteen persons were present at it." Consistent with the Christian view, Brand dismissed the notion that seating 13 at a table was unlucky.

Even after unlucky 13 was firmly entrenched in Western culture in the mid-nineteenth century, the Church never turned its back on the benevolent 13 of Christ and his disciples. Nor did it waiver in its condemnation of unlucky 13 as a sin. None of this had much effect on the triskaidekaphobic public, whose perspective was neatly captured in the design of a famous mechanical clock in Danzig, Germany, which was a popular tourist attraction at the time. Every day at noon, a small door opened in the housing of the clock and Christ and eleven of his disciples filed in. Then the door closed. Judas was left on the doorstep until 1:00, when he, too, was finally admitted—the unlucky 13th to arrive at the table.

CHAPTER FIVE

Friday the 13th

The minute I opened his office door this morning he flew at me like a panther. I told him I had only dropped in on my rounds for an order, as they were running off right smart, and I didn't know but he might like to pick up some bargains. "Bargains!" he roared, "don't you know the day? Don't you know it is Friday, the 13th? Go back to that hell-pit and sell, sell, sell." "Sell what and how much?" I asked. "Anything, everything. Give the thieves every share they will take, and when they won't take any more, ram as much again down their crops until they spit up all they have been buying for the last three months!"

—Thomas W. Lawson, *Friday, the Thirteenth* (1907)

I HAD, OF COURSE, heard of the Friday the 13th superstition before I found *Miscellany*; I had grown up with it, and with the movie. It was hard to believe that a superstition that was so familiar and so embedded in our culture—and that *seemed* so ancient—did not exist until the twentieth century. I was ten when *Friday the 13th* came out. I didn't get to see it until several years later. By then, it had taken on mythological proportions; there is nothing quite as scary as something that is too scary for you to be allowed to see. As for the day itself, no matter how much the more worldly kids in my class—the ones who knew all the curses and slang and loved to try them out on the rest of us—tried to make Friday the 13th sound frightening, it never made much of an impression on me.

Given unlucky Friday the 13th's relatively short history, I hoped to discover precisely when and how it began. In the end, I met with more success than I had with unlucky 13 at a table. I also learned the answer to a question that had puzzled me: if the 13-at-a-table superstition was able to withstand the Thirteen Club's best efforts to kill it, who or what had accomplished what that powerful group could not? The answer, I discovered, was that 13 had killed 13. Over the course of the first half of the twentieth century, Friday the 13th gradually cannibalized 13 at a table until it became the predominant incarnation of unlucky 13 and the *new* most popular superstition in the world.

THE THIRTEEN CLUB AND UNLUCKY FRIDAY

Friday the 13th only emerged as an independent superstition in the twentieth century. Friday on its own, however, had long been considered an unlucky day. Like fear of 13, fear of Friday was inspired by the New Testament. Although there has been a lot of debate about the precise date of Jesus' death, all of the early accounts of the Crucifixion are in agreement that it took place on a Friday (the day of crucifixion in ancient Rome). This connection between unlucky 13 and unlucky Friday was well known in the nineteenth century. In 1852, *Notes and Queries* observed: "There is as little doubt that Friday is considered unlucky because it is the day of the Crucifixion, as that the belief of its being unlucky for thirteen to set down to a meal together owes its origin to the remembrance of the Last Supper." In the mid- and late-nineteenth century, belief in unlucky Friday was almost as pervasive as belief in unlucky 13. Given their shared source, it is likely that they fueled each other's popularity.

Beginning in 1887, under the leadership of Chief Ruler David McAdam, chief justice of the City Court, the Thirteen Club trained its sights on another prominent superstition: unlucky Friday. The club was convinced that the tradition of holding executions on Friday, which persisted in late-nineteenth-century America, was the key to the superstition's continued popularity. Considering that the sixth day of the week was popularly known as "hangman's day," they had a point. The Thirteen Club took the same pragmatic approach with Friday that they had with 13 at a table. Using their legal connections, they actively courted judges and encouraged them to begin executing criminals on other days of the week; when a judge took their suggestion, the club issued a public congratulations. At one monthly dinner, the club celebrated the hanging of a convicted murderer that had taken place on a Thursday instead of a Friday. The sentencing judge, a colleague of Chief Ruler McAdam, explained in a letter read out loud at the dinner, "I thought it was time the slanders against Friday were stopped, and that the other days of the week should have their fair share of blame." Judges who sentenced men to hang on other days of the week were honored guests at Thirteen Club dinners, which at that time often carried with it the possibility of having one's name appear in the papers.

The Thirteen Club also assaulted unlucky Friday on another front. For some time the club had been a vocal supporter of the Half Holiday movement, a national campaign to make Saturday a half-holiday instead of a full workday—the convention at the time. One of the main arguments in favor of the Saturday half-holiday was that it would improve morale and morals among the working class by allowing them more time to prepare for Sunday's religious observances. In May 1887, a limited half-holiday law was enacted in New York State, but it applied only to banks and public offices. The Thirteen Club continued to campaign in the press for a more comprehensive law that would give "workingmen" similar rights. Issues of social welfare aside, the club wanted a more comprehensive half-holiday law as a first step toward making Saturday a full holiday. It was betting that if Friday was made the last day of the workweek, it would stop being associated with bad luck. The last day of the workweek is never unlucky—it is payday and the beginning of the holiday. It is also the last opportunity to accomplish the week's work goals, which means that the superstitious would not be able to stay home and hide under the covers. The ubiquitous expression *Thank God It's Friday* and the acronymic restaurant chain prove that their instincts were right.

In a speech at a Thirteen Club dinner in 1890, Judge McAdam summed up the club's role to date in reversing Friday's reputation: "Now anybody can have as much pleasure on that day as on any other, while those who were formerly hanged only on Friday may now have the pleasure of being hanged on every day of the week." An article in the *New York Times* two years later confirmed that, "Owing principally to the efforts of the Thirteen Club the execution day has been changed or varied in all States of the Union and thus has, to a great extent, brightened the day." Although the Thirteen Club enjoyed concrete success in its effort to change public perception of unlucky Friday, the superstition would, like unlucky 13 at a table, outlive its adversary, surviving until mid-century as a popular superstition independent of Friday the 13th.

THE RISE OF FRIDAY THE 13TH

In the late nineteenth and early twentieth centuries, the 13th day of every month was viewed as unlucky. This superstition emerged with the other 13 superstitions in the early nineteenth century. Friday the 13th was marginally unluckier than the other 13th days, but only because it combined two distinct unlucky superstitions: 13 and Friday. Evidence of this can be found in a grammatical peculiarity of the period: the fateful date always appeared in print as "Friday, the 13th." The comma denotes the fact that Friday and the 13th were perceived as separate phenomena.

It was during this time, before Friday the 13th emerged as a distinct superstition, that a third calendar event—Good Friday—briefly entered the mix. In the late nineteenth century, newspapers began to note when Good Friday fell on the 13th, and to highlight this as the unluckiest day possible, because it was the anniversary of Christ's crucifixion and it was the 13th. Fortunately for the superstitiously inclined, this was not a common occurrence: there was one in 1894 and not another until

VARIATIONS ON A THEME:
13 SUPERSTITIONS ABOUT FRIDAY THE 13TH

1

If a child is born on Friday the 13th, he will be unlucky all his life.

2

A child born on Friday the 13th will have a short life.

3

A child born on Friday the 13th will always be unlucky, but a part of this misfortune may be avoided by concealing the child's birthday.

4

A child born on Friday the 13th will not have any good luck until after the death of the last person who knows the true date of the child's birth.

5

A child born on Friday the 13th must carry a rabbit's foot
from a rabbit killed at midnight by a cross-eyed farmer.
Otherwise, the child will bring bad luck to the family.
If the child loses the rabbit's foot, he will die.

6

If a woman has a birthday on Friday the 13th,
she will marry and have a child within the year.

7

It is unlucky to be married on the 13th.

8

If a funeral procession passes a person on Friday the 13th,
he will be condemned to death.

9

Don't go out at night on Friday the 13th,
or you will have convulsions that night.

10

Don't sit 13 people at a table on Friday the 13th;
one will become seriously ill.

11

Don't cut your hair on Friday the 13th,
or someone in your family will die.

12

Don't wear black on Friday the 13th,
or you will soon wear it again in mourning.

13

It is good luck to be born on Friday the 13th.

1900. Perhaps the best evidence that Friday the 13th did not exist as an independent superstition in this period is the fact that the Thirteen Club never mentioned it—although they campaigned against both unlucky Friday and unlucky 13.

According to *A Dictionary of Superstitions* and other sources, the first reference to Friday the 13th as an independent superstition appeared in 1913, when a letter in *Notes and Queries* mentioned "the evil luck of Friday the 13th." Public opinion and almost every news story on Friday the 13th notwithstanding, contemporary folklorists are in agreement that Friday the 13th is a twentieth-century superstition. But no one has been able to pinpoint exactly when or why it emerged. In the first years of the twentieth century, newspaper articles on Thirteen Club dinners that took place on Friday the 13th continued to treat the two superstitions—unlucky Friday and the 13th day of the month—as distinct and separate beliefs. Often this was articulated with the convention of the comma—"Friday, the 13th." But at times the separation was made even more explicit. An article in the *New York Times* on June 14, 1902, began, "Taking advantage of Friday and the thirteenth day of the month, the Thirteen Club...gave a dinner last evening." Another, published on Friday, April 13, 1906, warning of the effects of superstition on Wall Street, observed, "To-day is Good Friday, also the 13th of the month...." An article the following day extolling the bravery of the Thirteen Club followed the same awkward practice: "The Great Unterrified, officially known as The Thirteen Club, met last night—the 13th, a Friday, and Good Friday at that...." Fletcher Bascom Dresslar's 1907 study on the superstitions of college students confirms that the following year Friday the 13th was still two separate superstitions—and that it was not very popular. Just 2 out of 1,875 students wrote: "If the 13th day of the month comes on a Friday, evil things are more likely to happen than at any other time," when asked to list all the superstitions with which they were familiar.

By 1908, however, Friday the 13th was sufficiently established to be acknowledged grammatically by the same paper that had not acknowledged its existence two years earlier: a *New York Times* article on March 14, 1908, began: "WASHINGTON, March 13.—Friday the 13th holds no terror for Senator Owen." (Owen had introduced 13 public building bills into the Senate that day for the state of Oklahoma.) The omission of the comma between *Friday* and *the* was not a typographical oversight; sometime between 1906 and 1908, *Friday, the 13th* became *Friday the 13th*. From this point on, more often than not the comma was avoided and newspapers dispensed with split references to the 13th day of the month and Friday, even on Good Friday.

By the second decade of the twentieth century, Friday the 13th was as well known as it is today. On Friday, April 13, 1917, a week after the United States declared war on Germany and entered World War I, New York City officials took a census of marriages. They were trying to determine if bachelors were getting married as a way of avoiding military service. On a date when few, if any, marriage licenses would normally be issued, 276 licenses were issued in Manhattan alone. This was considered proof positive that the recent trend of "connubial slackers" was still alive and well, despite a series of editorials and comments by public officials condemning the practice as unpatriotic and cowardly. It also amounts to official government acknowledgment of the prevalence of the Friday the 13th superstition in the second decade of the twentieth century.

The mystery of the missing comma in the *New York Times* narrowed my search for the point in time when unlucky Friday the 13th first emerged. It also pushed back the first known reference to the superstition from 1913 to 1908. I wondered what could have happened between 1906 and 1908 to put Friday the 13th on the path to becoming the most popular superstition of the twentieth century. I found my answer in the Thirteen Club's annual report for 1907. At the bottom of an advertisement for a Thirteen Club dinner on Friday, April 13, there was the following acknowledgment: "The thanks of the Club are due to Mr. Thomas W. Lawson who so kindly permitted us to use his day for our dinner."

I thought I detected jealousy in the Thirteen Club's sarcasm—as if Mr. Thomas W. Lawson were stealing its thunder. It turned out that this was exactly what had happened.

If one forgotten iconoclast—Captain Fowler—deserves credit for the Thirteen Club's impact on unlucky 13 and unlucky Friday in the nineteenth century, another—Thomas W. Lawson—deserves credit for guiding the course of both in the twentieth century. A successful, eccentric Boston financier and stock speculator who earned the nickname of "Copper King," Lawson was the author of several diatribes against stock speculation, the most successful of which was a book called *Frenzied Finance*, which appeared in 1905. Two years later, Lawson published his only novel, *Friday, the Thirteenth*. Although completely forgotten today, it was this novel that redefined the coincidence of unlucky Friday and the 13th as one superstition, and launched Friday the 13th in the popular imagination. Lawson kept the superstition front and center from the opening sentence—"Friday the 13th; I thought as much"—to its dramatic conclusion—"I staggered to his side. As I touched his now fast-icing brow my eyes fell upon the great black headlines spread across the top of the paper that Beulah Sands had been reading when the all-kind God had cut her bonds: FRIDAY THE THIRTEENTH. . . . "

Part torrid love story, part polemic on the crookedness of the "stock-gambling game," with a plot that hinged on a speculator's attempt to manipulate the market on Friday the 13th, *Friday, the Thirteenth* was as successful as it was awful. It sold 27,500 copies its first week in print, and after a month it had sold 60,000 copies. Sales were helped along by the provocative title and the author's celebrity, but his shameless self-promotion is what put the book over the top. Prior to publication, Lawson took out a series of advertisements in New York newspapers touting his "Big Novel." The day of publication he paid for a full-page ad in the *New York Times*, which included the following prediction: "A novel which will surely reach its hundreds of thousands of readers, men and women, quickly . . . A book which is going to make history; the author is convinced that it shows a perfectly simple yet inevitable way by which any broker with nerve enough can pull down the pillars of the Wall Street structure." The key to *Friday, the Thirteenth*'s sales, however, was the following bit of brilliant, if unscrupulous, marketing, which was also featured in the ad: "He has offered $5,000 to anyone who can show a flaw in his theory."

Less than two months later, Lawson and *Friday, the Thirteenth* made headlines when a stockbroker was arrested after attempting to derail the Philadelphia Stock Market by applying the novel's flawless theory.

When Friday the 13th made its next appearance on the calendar that September, Lawson created his own headline: he ran a large ad in the financial section of the *New York Times* that began:

FRIDAY THE 13TH

IT'S HERE TO-DAY

Lawson admonished readers to buy stock in companies in which he had a vested interest. His argument was that Wall Street's triskaidekaphobia would drive stock prices down, making it the perfect day to buy. His advertisements for his novel and this ad, all of which ran in 1907, are the earliest-known articulation in print of the Friday the 13th superstition as a superstition in its own right. They also represent the beginning of a long-standing tradition in advertising: the Friday the 13th ad.

The *Friday, the Thirteenth* phenomenon did not end there, however. The relationship between the motion picture and publishing industries in the early part of the twentieth century was not so different from the relationship between the two businesses today: a movie version of a book was both an indication of a book's success and an engine that drove further sales. In 1916, sixty-four years before the horror blockbuster *Friday the 13th* was released, *Friday the Thirteenth*, a feature-length silent version of Lawson's novel, complete with a new happy ending, written by future

Academy Award–winning screenwriter Frances Marion, made it to the big screen. Today, the film is lost; no prints are known to exist.

It was thanks to Thomas W. Lawson that *Friday, the 13th* became *Friday the 13th*; the tradition of unlucky Friday the 13th has not required any punctuation or qualifications ever since. Although forgotten today, Lawson's place in the history of unlucky 13 was acknowledged in his own lifetime. Two years before his death in 1925, at a time when his greatest successes—financial and literary—were in the distant past, Lawson received his due in a *New York Times* article that ran on Friday, April 13th: "A very substantial number of people may be found south of Fulton Street who would no more buy or sell a share of stock today than they would walk under a ladder or kick a black cat out of their path. The shades of Thomas W. Lawson continue to stalk through the canyons of Wall Street."

The connection between Friday the 13th and Wall Street has remained strong ever since. As recently as 1985, when the Dow Jones Industrial Average was struggling to break 1,300, there was talk on the Street that triskaidekaphobia was adding extra resistance to the psychological barrier the market normally encounters when it approaches the milestone of a round number—which is itself a number superstition. The longer it took to reach 1,300, and the more times it tried and failed—coming close, or reaching it intraday, only to drop back—the louder the talk became. In 1987, some traders saw a connection between the record 508-point decline on October 19—Black Monday—and the three Friday the 13ths that year—despite the fact that the Dow rose on two of those three days.

Friday, October 13, 1989, was definitely a bad day for the market: the Dow dropped 109 points, the largest one-day decline besides Black Monday. To make matters worse, the market had suffered a similar decline on the Friday before Black Monday, so a lot of traders spent that weekend in 1989 terrified that Black Monday might make a reappearance. In the end, the Dow rose 20-plus points on Monday. If it hadn't, who knows how much the reputation of Friday the 13th would have been enhanced. To this day, October is seen as a bad month for the stock market—which, naturally, tends to make it a bad month for the stock market.

BLACK CATS AND BELLS

By the 1930s, Friday the 13th was the most popular superstition in the country. A 1933 study in the *Journal of Abnormal Psychology* found that 95 percent of seniors and 91 percent of freshmen at seven midwestern colleges believed that "Friday the 13th always brings bad luck." The Friday the 13th superstition became so popular that it even infringed upon that hallowed ground of reason and rationality—the law—an accomplishment to which even 13 at a table could not lay claim. On Thursday, October 12, 1939, the town board of French Lick, Indiana, decreed that beginning at midnight and continuing for twenty-four hours, all the black cats in town had to wear bells, so residents could avoid them on the fateful day. An article in that day's *Indianapolis News* explained, "The board thinks there's enough bad luck in the world right now without black cats adding their share on Friday the 13th." The board assigned the town marshal with the task of belling the cats.

The timing of the decree, five weeks after the start of World War II, lends support to the popular theory that superstitions become more pronounced during times of uncertainty. The decree had enough public support that it stayed on the books through 1940. The board abandoned the practice in 1941, but a particularly unlucky Friday the 13th in June of that year led them to reinstate it for 1942. There is no information on when the tradition ended—whether, for example, it survived the war. It did continue at least through November 13, 1942; the *New York Times* picked up the story on November 11 of that year, calling the decree "a war measure to alleviate mental strain upon the populace."

THE POLITICS OF 13

The late nineteenth century marked a turning point for superstitions; for the first time, organized religion lost its exclusive claim as arbiter of superstitious beliefs. Prior to the twentieth century, most dictionaries followed the Church's lead and defined *superstition* as a vice contrary to religion by excess. In the new century, however, more and more dictionaries replaced this religious definition with a secular one: *superstition* became an irrational belief stemming from fear or ignorance. Where once superstition offended God, it now offended Reason. Later in the century, even the Catholic Church accepted a more secularized definition of superstition; in 1967, the first revised edition of the *Catholic Encyclopedia* defined superstition as any "irrational or abject attitude of mind toward the supernatural, nature, or God, proceeding from ignorance, unreasoning fear of the unknown or the mysterious, or from morbid scrupulosity." This shift set the stage for a new assault on unlucky 13 and Friday the 13th.

After World War II, politics replaced religion as the major adversary of superstition in the United States. In the wake of the Nazis' unprecedented exploitation of social prejudice, the public was actively discouraged from viewing superstitions as merely sinful or frivolous beliefs. Conventional superstitions like fear of 13, walking under ladders, black cats, and spilled salt were thought to originate from the same malevolent, irrational wellspring as the racial and ethnic prejudices that had been the justification for the Holocaust. Increasingly, the U.S. government (and the media) attacked superstitions as unpatriotic and unscientific, an open threat to democratic freedom and progress. There was a concerted national effort to educate the public about their dangers.

Part of that effort was the First American Exhibition on Superstition, Prejudice and Fear, which (not coincidentally) ran for 13 days at the American Museum of Natural History in Manhattan, beginning Friday, August 13, 1948. The exhibition borrowed freely from the Thirteen Club's bag of tricks: to enter, visitors had to pass underneath one of three giant ladders; a raft of open umbrellas was suspended from the ceiling; there were displays of spilled salt and broken mirrors, and silhouettes of black cats were taped to the walls. Posters underscored the perceived connection between superstition and prejudice: STOP DISCRIMINATION. WIPE OUT PREJUDICE. The museum collaborated with Columbia University's Department of Anthropology on an exhibit on race and racism, which included displays of primitive masks and rituals and a quiz on the differences among races.

As the date of its opening and the length of its run suggest, unlucky 13 was one of the primary targets of the exhibition. A prominent poster recalled the benevolent role of 13 in the nation's history: "13 is lucky... U.S. history proves it! Don't be superstitious!" According to the *New York Times*, the "most outstanding decoration of the show" was a 13-month calendar in which there was a Friday the 13th every month. The paper ran a large photograph of the "inventor" of the calendar with hammer in hand, tacking it to the wall. Stenciled on the calendar was the following:

VEMBO'S 13 MONTH WORLD CALENDAR
TO ERADICATE
fear of 13
TRISKAIDEKAPHOBIA

The calendar even predicted a date for "world adoption" of the 13-month calendar: Sunday, January 13, 1950. The inventor, misidentified in the article as "an Egyptian resident in New York," was the celebrated Greek contralto and anti-Nazi activist Sophia Vembo, who had made her Carnegie Hall debut the previous year. The brainchild of the exhibition was the National Committee of 13 Against Superstition and Fear, which was founded on April 13, 1946, by Nicholas Matsoukas, a prominent theater manager and a colleague of Sophia Vembo's.

If the title of the exhibition suggested that there would be further American Exhibitions on Superstition, Prejudice and Fear, there is no record of them. Nor is there any further record of the National Committee of 13 Against Superstition and Fear.

However, others continued the campaign. The 1952 book, *Understanding Public Opinion: A Guide for Newspapermen and Newspaper Readers*, not only captured the sentiments of the era, but also influenced a generation of journalists:

> [The superstitious person] not only has false hopes and fears, but he is a sucker for demagogic appeal. He is inclined toward racial prejudice, disregarding all anthropological evidence to the contrary, and in a time of insecurity he will fall for any kind of new Messiah that comes along.... A person who believes in black cats and umbrellas and all of these other everyday superstitions is less likely to think logically and clearly in any other field. He is continuing in an unscientific frame of mind at a time when the clearest type of scientific thinking is essential.

This hyperbole pales in comparison to a cheery 1960 article in the *New York Times*, "Atomic Survival Called Doubtful," which has preserved for posterity the period's bizarre overestimation of the dangers of superstition. The article covered a speech by Dr. Brock Chisholm, the former director general of the World Health Organization, to the National Conference on Social Work, in which he argued that eradicating superstition was one of the keys to the survival of mankind in the Atomic Age. His contention was that superstition impeded man's ability to face reality, which, in turn, restricted his ability to adapt to new threats, like the prospect of nuclear war:

The specialist observed that there was a good deal of "magic" that many people linked to survival—hotels without thirteenth floors, learned professors knocking on wood.... Man must learn to face reality in the unaccustomed role of self-survival today, and he can begin by eliminating superstition in his life.

Not even the Church, which viewed superstition as a minor sin—"a vain observance in daily life"—put as much emphasis on the need for its elimination.

In the postwar years, there were two types of newspaper coverage of unlucky 13: articles like those on the Museum of Natural History exhibit and the National Conference on Social Work, which supported the contention that superstition was a serious social disease, and the next generation of the gently mocking commentary that had been pioneered in the days of the Thirteen Club. With the Thirteen Club and its monthly dinners a thing of the past, journalists came to rely on the periodic reappearance of Friday the 13th to generate coverage of the superstition. *Understanding Public Opinion* had no sympathy for this journalistic tradition: "The Friday the 13th feature is, of course, almost a 'must' in every newspaper office.... Reporters often strain themselves to get a '13' story."

The following year, in 1953, the *New York Times* published the prototype for many of today's Friday the 13th stories—"Friday, the B-r-r-r!" Calling it "the most widespread of all superstitions," the article warned the public that 1953 was going to have three Friday the 13ths—each year has between one and three—

making it "a terrible one for triskaidekaphobes." The article is one of the few to quantify the impact of Friday the 13th on our culture: "Any Friday the 13th, it is estimated, costs the nation $250,000,000 in business loss." Presumably, this meant that in 1953, Friday the 13th was going to drain the economy of $750 million—although there was no information on how this estimate was determined.

"Friday, the B-r-r-r!" proved to be an influential story. The $250 million figure has been quoted in articles ever since, often without regard to the passage of time or the possibility that Friday the 13th's impact may not have remained constant over the years. "Friday, the B-r-r-r!" contains the first reference in the *New York Times* to the theory that unlucky 13 may have begun with the death of Baldur in Norse mythology. The wording of the Baldur references in subsequent Friday the 13th articles suggests that most journalists came to the theory via this article rather than directly from Cobham Brewer's *Dictionary of Phrase and Fable*.

For the next twenty-five years, Friday the 13th was nearly as regular an event in newspapers as it was on the calendar. Both types of coverage—critical and irreverent—helped to ensure that public awareness of the Friday the 13th superstition remained nearly universal, while at the same time undercutting actual belief in the superstition. Meanwhile, there were fewer and fewer references in the media to unlucky 13 at a table. The once-great superstition was able to withstand the sustained attack of the Thirteen Club but not the politicization of unlucky 13, the shift in media attention to Friday the 13th, and the emergence of alternative theories about the origin of unlucky 13. People no longer remembered that 13 at a table was the original 13 superstition, or that it was inspired by the Last Supper—which deprived it of much of its potency. Dethroned and disconnected from its roots, in the span of one generation 13 at a table went from being the most powerful 13 superstition to the most vulnerable. Of all the 13 superstitions, it was the easiest to disprove; there was nothing vague about the assertion that if 13 people sat at a table one would die within a year. While the public, spurred on by the calendar and the Friday the 13th newspaper feature, focused on the unlucky date, 13 at a table slowly faded away.

THE MOVIE

In 1980, two ambitious filmmakers, producer/director Sean S. Cunningham and screenwriter Victor Miller, collaborated on a horror film called *Long Night at Camp Blood*. The plot was straightforward and effective. In 1958, two camp counselors are murdered at Camp Crystal Lake. The murderer is never found and the camp is eventually closed. Twenty-two years later, the new camp owner and counselors are preparing to reopen Camp Crystal Lake (nicknamed by the locals "Camp Blood"). One by one, the camp's owner and counselors are stalked and killed by an unseen murderer. At the end of the movie, the killer is revealed to be the mother of Jason Voorhees, a young boy who drowned at the camp in 1957.

It was Sean Cunningham who suggested changing the title of the film to *Friday the 13th*, a move calculated to imitate the calendar-driven 1978 mega-hit *Halloween*. Victor Miller loved the new title and added some dialogue to make the action take place on Friday the 13th. Neither man was triskaidekaphobic or had any inherent interest in the 13 superstition. Both have acknowledged that the decision to change the title was one of the key factors that made *Friday the 13th* one of the most successful horror movie franchises in history. Victor Miller has described it as being "immensely important" to the success of the film. To date, there have been ten sequels:

Friday the 13th Part 2 (1981)

Friday the 13th Part 3: 3D (1982)

Friday the 13th: The Final Chapter (1984)

Friday the 13th: A New Beginning (1985)

Friday the 13th Part VI: Jason Lives (1986)

Friday the 13th Part VII: The New Blood (1988)

Friday the 13th Part VIII: Jason Takes Manhattan (1989)

Jason Goes To Hell: The Final Friday (1993)

Jason X (2002)

Freddy vs. Jason (2003)

Since 1980, *Friday the 13th* has become a central reference point for triskaidekaphobes and triskaidekaphiles—one of the things people always mention when the subject of 13 comes up. But unlike Thomas W. Lawson's *Friday, the Thirteenth*, Sean S. Cunningham's *Friday the 13th* does not appear to have increased the overall prevalence of the Friday the 13th superstition in the United States. The politicization of 13 and superstition had taken its toll. What the films and its sequels did do, however, was help spread awareness of the unlucky Friday the 13th superstition throughout the world. In some countries, Friday the 13th took root for the first time—and a new cultural superstition was born. Three-quarters of a century after Thomas W. Lawson's "Big Novel" created unlucky Friday the 13th from two distinct super- stitions—unlucky 13 and unlucky Friday—a single individual who was not superstitious had again altered the course of the world's most popular superstition.

MORE 13 MOVIES

1 *License No. 13, or The Hoodoo Automobile* (1905)

2 *The Thirteen Club* (1905)

3 *Thirteen at Table* (1907)

4 *A Jar of Cranberry Sauce, or The Crime in Room 13* (1910)

5 *The Thirteenth Man* (1913)

6 *The Mystery of Room 13* (1915)

7 *The Rise and Fall of Officer 13* (1915)

8 *The Thirteenth Girl* (1916)

9 *The Thirteenth Chair* (1919)

10 *The Woman in Room 13* (1920)

11 *Number 13* (1922)

12 *Bell Boy 13* (1923)

13 *The Thirteenth Man* (1926)

1 *Taxi 13* (1928)

2 *13 Washington Square* (1928)

3 *The Thirteenth Chair* (1929)

4 *The Night of June 13* (1932)

5 *Officer 13* (1932)

6 *Thirteen Steps* (1932)

7 *Thirteen Women* (1932)

8 *The Thirteenth Guest* (1932)

9 *The Woman in Room 13* (1932)

10 *Friday the 13th* (1934)

11 *Operator 13* (1934)

12 *13 Hours by Air* (1936)

13 *The Thirteenth Chair* (1937)

1 *The 13th Man* (1937)

2 *Black Friday*, or *Friday the Thirteenth* (1940)

3 *Pier 13* (1940)

4 *The Mystery of the 13th Guest* (1943)

5 *13 Rue Madeleine* (1947)

6 *The 13th Hour* (1947)

7 *Bungalow 13* (1948)

8 *13 Lead Soldiers* (1948)

9 *Highway 13* (1949)

10 *I Married a Communist*, or *The Woman on Pier 13* (1950)

11 *The 13th Letter* (1951)

12 *The Hour of 13* (1952)

13 *13 East Street* (1952)

1. *13 Ghosts* (1960)
2. *Girl in Room 13* (1961)
3. *13 West Street* (1962)
4. *Dementia 13* (1963)
5. *13 Frightened Girls* (1963)
6. *Eye of the Devil,* or *13* (1967)
7. *Assault on Precinct 13* (1976)
8. *Apollo 13* (1995)
9. *Redboy 13* (1997)
10. *The Thirteenth Floor* (1999)
11. *The 13th Warrior* (1999)
12. *Thirteen Ghosts* (2001)
13. *13th Child* (2002)

The beginning of the Thirteen Club. From the cover of the first Thirteen Club Annual Report, 1882.

Thirteen Club logos. From the Thirteen Club Annual Report, 1886.

From the cover of the Thirteen Club Annual Report, 1892.

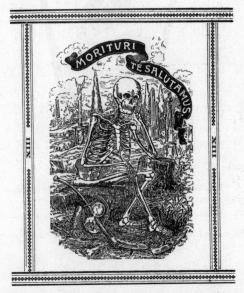

From the cover of the Thirteen Club Annual Report, 1893.

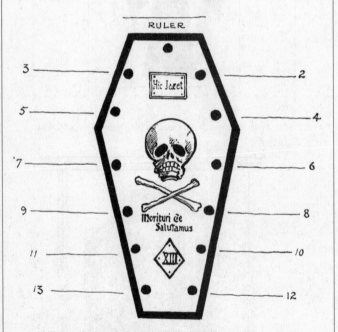

This card is given to each diner, who has it filled out with the autographs of those at the same table, and preserves it as a souvenir.

Hic jacet is Latin for "Here lies." Thirteen Club Annual Report, 1901.

FRONT OF MENU CARD.
ONE-QUARTER ACTUAL SIZE.

BACK OF MENU CARD.
ONE-QUARTER ACTUAL SIZE.

From the Thirteen Club Annual Report, 1902.

From the Thirteen Club Annual Report, 1906.

In the early twentieth century, African Americans were often characterized as the most superstitious population in the country. This was usually cast in racist terms; their superstitions were attributed to their being less intelligent and more primitive than their Caucasian counterparts. The cartoonist Frederick Opper created several famous early newspaper strips, including *Happy Hooligan, Alphonse and Gaston,* and *Maud the Mule*—the star of the cartoon above. Thirteen Club Annual Report, 1906.

In 1907, newspaper cartoonist Gene Carr—the creator of *Lady Bountiful,* the first strip to feature a heroine—drew a series of cartoons depicting members of the Thirteen Club acting out popular superstitions. From TOP LEFT to LOWER RIGHT: Friday is an unlucky day; breaking a mirror brings seven years of bad luck; if friends are separated, the friendship will soon end; spilling salt brings bad luck. Thirteen Club Annual Report, 1907.

Three more cartoons in the series by Gene Carr. UPPER LEFT: It is bad luck to open an umbrella inside. The large bone J. P. Scrymser is holding probably represents a rifle. A captain in the Thirteenth Regiment, Scrymser was a prominent member of the Veteran's Military Rifle Association of New York. UPPER RIGHT: It is unlucky to see the new moon over your left shoulder. BOTTOM: If you put your clothes on inside out, keep them that way, or you will have bad luck. John F. Hobbes was chief ruler of the Thirteen Club in New York, and a king in the South Pacific. Thirteen Club Annual Report, 1907.

RESOLVED
CIRCUMSTANTIAL EVIDENCE
SHOWS THAT 13 IS N'T UNLUCKY
THERE IS NO SUCH THING AS LUCK
WHEN YOU BELIEVE IN LUCK YOU'RE IN
A BAD FIX. GOD MADE YOU, BELIEVE
IN YOURSELF AND HUSTLE. THEN
LUCK, GOOD OR BAD, WON'T BOTHER
YOU. HOW COULD THERE BE ANY SUCH
THING AS LUCK? DONT LET US BE
PINHEADS; YOU MIGHT AS WELL
BELIEVE THERE'S A SATAN AND
A HELL. BUSTER BROWN

To The 13 Club
with the sincere regards
R.F. Outcault
Friday Sep 13th
1907.

XX

R. F. Outcault was the creator of *The Yellow Kid*, the world's first cartoon strip, and *Buster Brown*. Both strips were enormously successful and helped establish the tradition of comic strip merchandizing. Thirteen Club Annual Report, 1907.

Twenty-three skiddoo was a popular expression in the early twentieth century, meaning "go away" or "get lost"; sometimes the expression was shortened to "twenty-three." Its origin is obscure. In the 1920s, the cartoonist Charles W. Bowers became a successful silent film writer-director-actor and a master of innovative film animation techniques. Thirteen Club Annual Report, 1907.

Photograph of Thomas W. Lawson, author of the 1907 novel *Friday, the Thirteenth* and the person responsible for the Friday the 13th superstition. Library of Congress.

New York Times advertisement, February 26, 1907. This was one of a number of ads that ran in the *Times* that year promoting Lawson's novel.

CHAPTER SIX

The Missing 13

Elevator rides are, for the most part, short, so don't forget to begin your mingling when you are waiting for the elevator.... "Is there a thirteenth floor in this building? No? Isn't it amazing how that superstition seems to prevail?"

—Jeanne Martinet, *The Art of Mingling:*

Easy, Fun, and Proven Techniques for Mastering Any Room (1992)

F RIDAY THE 13TH was not the only unlucky 13 to first take hold in the twentieth century. There was also the architectural phenomenon of the missing 13th floor. The proliferation of the skyscraper in the twentieth century gave the superstition one of its most public symbols. While most incarnations of unlucky 13 were transient—13 guests at a table, 13 coins in a pocket, the 13th day of the month—the missing 13th floor phenomenon was a constant, objective reminder of the prevalence of the superstition. In the late nineteenth century, when the skyscraper was still in its infancy, people were already avoiding homes and offices with the number 13 in their address. Triskaidekaphobia was so prevalent at the time that buildings that predated the superstition or that had deigned to ignore it were being renumbered. In 1900, the newly elected New York City controller discovered that his predecessor had changed the office's number from 13 to 14. An honorary member of the Thirteen Club, he promptly had the 14 changed back to 13, explaining at the next monthly dinner that he did not want to "sail under false colors." Before hotels had 13 floors, they were skipping Room 13s. Because it was common knowledge that many triskaidekaphobes interpreted any number with a 13 in it—e.g., 713—as unlucky, more and more hotels purged their rooms of all 13s. Unfortunately for hoteliers, triskaidekaphobes also tended to fear numbers that added up to 13; to them, Room 454 was just a camouflaged Room 13.

As early as 1903, Manhattan's tall buildings were omitting the 13th floor. For a time, new buildings in the Wall Street area were more likely to omit the 13th floor than buildings in other parts of Manhattan—a response to the superstitious tendencies of tenants whose livelihood depended upon the vicissitudes of the stock market. But by the arrival of the office-building boom of the 1920s and early 1930s, the 13th floor was omitted from most new tall buildings in New York. (There have always been exceptions to the 13th floor omission; for example, the most famous New York building from this period, the Empire State Building, has a 13th floor.) The rest of the country followed New York's lead. Not only were new buildings around the country missing 13th floors, but the 13th floors in some older buildings were also eliminated. After taking over a new property, it was not uncommon for new management to rename the unlucky floor (and all room numbers containing 13) as one of their first official acts of business.

The missing 13th floor has always been an especially common phenomenon in hotels—a setting in which people experience the anxiety of sleeping in a new environment, surrounded by strangers, and where turnover is high (increasing the chances of triskaidekaphobic guests). Most articles on unlucky 13 mention the absence of 13th floors in hotels as evidence of the prevalence of the superstition today. One morning, I decided to call a few New York hotels to gauge exactly how common this tradition was. A manager at the first one I contacted, the Parker Meridien, informed me matter-of-factly that "There are no hotels in New York with a 13th floor. None at all." That gave me an incentive to find one. When I called the Four Seasons Hotel, the woman who answered the phone told me they didn't have one either, and added, "It's bad luck!" The Stanhope didn't have a 13th floor. Neither did the Sherry-Netherland (they used to have Suite 13s, but encountered enough triskaidekaphobes that they changed the numbers in the mid-1950s). Staff at hotel after hotel assured me they did not have a 13th floor—until a manager at the Carleton expressed confidence that they had one, put me on hold, then returned to tell me that they didn't after all. But in the end I was triumphant: The Waldorf-Astoria has a 13th floor. What's more, it has always had one.

No one has ever conducted an exhaustive survey of 13th-floor omission in U.S. architecture. From time to time, however, there have been articles on the evolution of the tradition. In 1958, a *New York Times* article, "13th Floor Losing Its Absence Here," claimed that the missing-13th-floor tradition had undergone a transformation in the postwar years. New office buildings were including the 13th floor more often, but new apartment buildings were still as diligent as ever in omitting it. According to the article, this new pattern reflected a significant gender split on unlucky 13; in a section headed "Women Scorn '13,'" the article quoted a prominent builder of the day:

> Business men today are too sophisticated. If they find the space they want, they'll take it no matter how the floor is designated. On the other hand, in renting a new apartment, the final word is usually given to the woman of the house. And I've found that women are still likely to be influenced by a dislike of the thirteenth floor.

THE MISSING 13TH FLOOR TODAY

To learn more about the missing 13th floor today, I contacted architects and developers at the top one hundred U.S. firms. Most reported that they still omit the 13th floor, whether the project is an office or an apartment building. Not surprisingly, none of them blamed the persistence of the tradition on the superstitious nature of women. In the opinion of Ev Ruffcorn, a design partner at Zimmer Gunsul Frasca in Portland, Oregon, who has designed a number of high-rise office buildings, there are two reasons for the persistence of 13th-floor omission. First, developers want to eliminate all impediments to securing tenants; and second, building owners want the tallest building possible (the height of a building is denoted by its tallest floor). Architects have observed the same trend in residential apartment buildings. The client's goal is maximum occupancy at the highest rent possible. Since few people seek out a 13th-floor address, and an unknown percentage avoid it, the prudent developer follows the convention. From an economic perspective, omitting the 13th floor has advantages beyond the risk of ignoring the superstitions of the marketplace: the higher the floor the greater the status—and the more expensive the lease.

Usually, during construction on a building, everyone refers to the 13th floor as the *13th floor*. A lot of times the floor is even labeled *13* temporarily to keep communication simple and to reduce the chance of costly mistakes. Only after the building is completed is the floor renamed. The persistence of the missing-13th-floor tradition means that for every building with 13 or more floors going up in the United States today, at some point a conversation will take place between architect and client about triskaidekaphobia. Zimmer Gunsul Frasca broaches the subject in the final stages of design, when the issue of signage usually comes up. In Ev Ruffcorn's experience, the conversation is almost always the same: "We discuss the pros and cons. And then eliminate the 13th floor." To date, no client has ever insisted on having a 13th floor, or, for that matter, admitted to believing in the superstition. Similarly, none of the architects I talked with said that they believed that the 13th floor was inherently unlucky. Thirteenth-floor omission is always about what other people believe, or *may* believe.

The contemporary architect's approach to 13th-floor omission is completely insensitive to the actual status of unlucky 13 in our culture; belief in the superstition could fade to nothing, and the inertia of the better-safe-than-sorry approach would keep the convention alive. This is of more than passing significance to the story of 13 because the missing 13th floor is one of the few concrete manifestations of the superstition in our culture; every skyscraper elevator without a 13 button is a reminder of the phenomenon of unlucky 13. As such, it exerts a profound influence on public perception. Ask someone to assess the prevalence of triskaidekaphobia in our culture, and he will invariably mention the missing-13th-floor phenomenon as indisputable evidence of its hold on us. After all, architecture is an intrinsically rational and scientific occupation involving precise calculations and measurements; what architect would go out of his way to do something so ridiculous unless there were millions of terrified triskaidekaphobes out there?

The public tends to interpret 13th-floor omission as evidence not only that there is a multitude of triskaidekaphobes among us, but also that they must be pretty dim-witted. There is a general consensus—echoed in many newspaper stories about unlucky 13—that relabeling the 13th floor is ridiculous because no matter what one calls it, it is still 13 floors up from the ground. Even great and generous minds are guilty of this unfortunate slander against the triskaidekaphobe. Writing on superstition in *Strength to Love*, Martin Luther King, Jr. approvingly quotes an elevator man who tells him, "The real foolishness of the fear is to be found in the fact that the fourteenth floor is actually the thirteenth." This common perspective on the 13th-floor superstition ignores the iconic power the number 13 has over the triskaidekaphobe. In the case of the 13th floor, there is evidence that he perceives the label *13th floor*—not the floor itself—to be the source of the bad luck. The architectural tradition of the ground floor provides a good test case. In highrises where there is both a ground floor and a 1st floor, and the 13th floor is not omitted, the triskaidekaphobe has to decide which floor to avoid: the designated 13th floor (14 floors up) or the designated 12th floor (13 floors up). Faced with this choice, the triskaidekaphobe will avoid the floor that is labeled the 13th floor. This is why the architectural tradition of the missing 13th floor is an effective strategy for minimizing the anxiety and potential financial impact of unlucky 13—not because triskaideka-phobes are any less intelligent than the rest of the public.

OTHER MISSING 13s

Thirteen has never been avoided in street addresses as assidu-ously as it has in floor designations—which may reflect the added fears associated with skyscrapers when they were still a new architectural milestone. While it is true that on the odd side of many residential streets there is no house number 13—including the street on which I live—there are still lots of homes for triskaidekaphiles. According to Melissa Data Corp., the five most popular street names in the United States, in descending order, are Main, Washington, Park, Broadway, and Maple. A triskai-dekaphilic Manhattanite who is tired of the missing 13th floors, and in search of a new home, will find no fewer thirty 13 Main Streets within thirty miles of midtown, or, if he prefers some-thing more picturesque, no fewer than twenty-eight 13 Maple

Streets. Thirteenth Street and 13th Avenue have also always had a much more consistent presence in the United States than the 13th floor. Manhattan has a 13th Street, as do many U.S. cities: Chicago, Boston, Washington, D.C., Birmingham, Dallas, Indianapolis, San Francisco, Boise, Bangor, Jacksonville, Cleveland, and Lincoln, Nebraska, to name a handful. In Santa Monica, a rare exception, the street between 12th and 14th is called Euclid. New Orleans is another exception; there, the street after 12th is 14th Street. Avenues labeled 13th are more unusual, but only because fewer cities have numbered avenues. Los Angeles and Portland are both examples of cities that have 13th Avenues.

It is fitting that a superstition that began as the mortally unlucky 13 at a table would make its presence felt where the dead are laid to rest. Matthews International Corporation of Pittsburgh, Pennsylvania, a 150-year-old company that designs community mausoleums, reports that about half of the cemetery owners they work with request that they skip crypts and caskets numbered 13, "Because people won't buy a final resting place for their loved one that bears the number 13." It is not clear who customers think the bad luck would descend upon if they purchased number 13—themselves or the deceased. Or perhaps they feel that it would convey a lack of respect for the departed. As in the case of the 13th floor, with mausoleums it is the label 13 itself that is significant; customers do not avoid the 13th crypt or casket in a row when it is assigned another number.

The unlucky 13 that dogged the high seas in the nineteenth century extended its reach to include the newest and riskiest mode of transportation—the airplane—in the twentieth century. The 1925 English book *Popular Superstitions* articulates the fear and uncertainty of air travel in its early days:

> Airmen nowadays are very superstitious, and it certainly is strange that so many fatal accidents should have occurred on the thirteenth of the month. Very few airmen will now ascend on that day. A really extraordinary series of such accidents occurred in March, April, May, July, August, September and October 1912—in May, two men were killed in distinct accidents. This sequence of fatalities continued in the January and February of 1913, but after that it ceased because the men refused to run the risk.

This early fear eventually translated into the practice of omitting Row 13 on commercial airplanes. For decades, Row 13 omission has, like the missing 13th floor, been taken as concrete evidence of the superstition's prevalence. Recent newspaper articles continue to claim that most airplanes do not have a 13th row and to draw the same inference. Today, however, airlines such as American, Delta, Northwest, United, Jet Blue, and Alaskan Airways include a Row 13 in all their planes—other than when design specifications (e.g., the placement of lavatories and service stations) require its omission as part of a block of skipped rows. In fact, the only major U.S. carrier that still omits Row 13 on all its planes, domestic and international, is Continental; every plane in their fleet jumps from Row 12 to Row 14. When I asked a Continental spokeswoman the reason for this, she told me they were not aware that other carriers now had Row 13s. She added: "It was omitted a long time ago and there has never been a reason to reinstate it. We have no plans to change from the current numbering."

Another U.S. airline that shows a residual trace of triskaidekaphobia is US Airways. They include Row 13 on all their planes except the Canadair Regional Jet, a small plane that includes exactly 13 rows of seats. Because this airplane's design specifications call for 13 rows, if airlines elect to number the rows sequentially, the result is a 13-row airplane with a designated Row 13—a double-13 effect. This apparently proved too much for US Airways; their Canadair Regional Jet is the only plane in their fleet that skips from 12 to 14, making it a 13-row plane without a Row 13. Northwest and United apparently are less concerned about triskaidekaphobic customers; their Canadair Regional Jets both end with Row 13.

OTHER BUILDING SUPERSTITIONS

The missing 13th floor and Room 13 are the most famous building superstitions in Western culture, but they are not the only ones. Many people avoid purchasing a home in which a previous occupant was murdered or committed suicide—the starting point for many a horror movie. Other superstitions that have not survived as long as 13 include the belief that one should always move one's office to a higher floor rather than a lower floor (which also emerged with the skyscraper), and the once-common practice of not breaking ground on a new building on a Friday—back when

Friday was seen as an unlucky day. Building superstitions of more ancient origin include laying laths crosswise under a new construction to ward off the devil and, in mid-nineteenth-century England, the belief that a person could not die peacefully under the crossbeam of a house.

The Asian tradition of feng shui—the arrangement of objects in the home to bring the space into harmony with nature and spiritual forces—has been an occasional influence on U.S. architecture at least since the 1970s. But in recent years feng shui has become a significant design force in corporate as well as residential architecture, especially in the Western United States. According to a number of large U.S. architectural firms, more and more clients are requesting that a feng shui master review the designs; some firms have even retained feng shui consultants on an ongoing basis. The architects I talked with took this development in stride. Even those who dismissed it as a superstition were all too familiar with the vagaries of client demands and are usually willing to accommodate them.

Feng shui is not the only architectural tradition today that draws on the alleged mystical implications of architectural space. The Estonians, for example, believe that there are hidden waterways underground that influence the harmony of a building and the well being of its occupants. According to a representative at the Estonian Embassy in Washington, D.C.: "Many Estonians can 'feel' the waterways beneath the land. If there is a waterway, it is important that one's bed is not placed over it. It is also very bad to have one's desk or any sitting place over a natural well." There is an interesting combination of politics and superstition in the

Estonian tradition: "Old Estonian farmhouses were generally built in a good natural spot; the Soviet buildings that went up postwar paid no attention to underground water systems and in addition to being ugly and poorly built, they just don't have a good 'feel' to them." Unfortunately for the Estonians, their belief in the significance of underground waterways has not traveled as well as feng shui. Over the past decade, U.S. publishers have put out hundreds of books extolling the virtues of feng shui. To date, not one book has been published in the United States promoting Estonian architectural superstitions. At least it gets a mention here.

Unlike Friday the 13th, the missing 13th floor and the other missing 13s in architecture and design have never emerged as revisionist contenders for the original 13 superstition. This is probably because their history is so closely tied to two of the most famous symbols of modernity: the skyscraper and the airplane. Their role today, however, in the story of the world's most popular superstition is no less significant than that of Friday the 13th. They keep alive the belief that untold millions suffer from triskaidekaphobia. As long as there are buildings that omit the 13th floor and as long as newspapers continue to claim that all airplanes omit Row 13, the public will continue to assume that unlucky 13 is one of the most popular superstitions in our culture.

CHAPTER SEVEN

The Psychology of 13

Take, for instance, a dream in which the number 13 occurs. . . .

—Carl Jung, *Man and His Symbols* (1964)

THE TWENTIETH CENTURY'S third major contribution to the phenomenon of unlucky 13 was a new word: *triskaideka-phobia*—excessive or morbid fear of the number 13. *Triskaideka-phobia* appears on most of the favorite- and unusual-word lists that are published in newspapers and online. Lots of people claim it is their favorite word. Back in the early 1980s, not long after the movie *Friday the 13th* came out, research librarians at the New York Public Library reported that one of the questions they were asked most often was "What is the word for fear of 13?" For many people today, that is what *triskaidekaphobia* has devolved into—a word for trivia connoisseurs. But this has not always been the case. There was a time when *triskaidekaphobia* was a diagnosis.

Newspaper sources claim that *triskaidekaphobia* was coined by Isador H. Coriat, M.D., an American neurologist and psychoanalyst, and that it appeared for the first time in his 1910 book, *Abnormal Psychology*. In the book, the word itself is accorded no special favor; "fear of the number thirteen (triskaidekaphobia)" appears in a short list of "the more common fears," between "fear of dirt or germs (mygophobia)" and "fear of railroads (sideropho-bia)." Given its indifferent treatment, it is unlikely that this was the occasion of *triskaidekaphobia*'s invention or inauguration into print. This is probably fortunate, since Dr. Coriat wasn't much of an authority on etymology—or on spelling. *Mygophobia*, fear of germs or dirt, is actually spelled *mysophobia*, and *siderophobia* means fear of stars, not railroads or trains (that distinction is held by the word *siderodromophobia*).

In the early years of the twentieth century, there was much less unanimity about the diagnosis and treatment of mental illnesses than there is today. Coriat's book was one of a number of attempts to arrive at a general classification system for mental illness. Writing within the psychoanalytic tradition, he characterized phobias as "systematized emotional agita-tions," part of a myriad of symptoms, most anxiety-related, that made up a category of mental illnesses called "psychasthenia." Like countless other psychiatric diagnoses over the years, *psy-chasthenia* has become a victim of progress; according to the *American Heritage Dictionary*, *psychasthenia* is "no longer in scientific use."

Historically, phobias have been of greater interest to psychoanalysis than to other schools of therapy. It is not surprising that the first published use of *triskaidekaphobia* is credited to a psychoanalyst. For the psychoanalyst, a patient's phobia is—inevitably—a doorway that leads to the discovery of deeper, more profound problems that are the real source of the patient's troubles. At its most extreme, psychoanalysis can make numerology seem like a science by comparison. By way of example, consider this excerpt from a psychoanalytic analysis of a patient who feared all even numbers and the numbers 21 and 23, which appeared in the *International Journal of Psycho-Analysis* in 1938: "Analysis revealed that repressed genitality, first made conscious traumatically at the age of 18, accounted for the fear of the number 18, and that likewise a complicated Oedipus situation was symbolized by the other numbers, with 2 . . . essentially giving expression to Oedipus impulses." The interest among psychoanalysts in number symbolism can be traced back to the father of psychoanalysis, Sigmund Freud, who in *The Interpretation of Dreams* (1900) declared, "We have . . . abundant confirmation that the figure three is a symbol of the male genitals."

Charles Brenner's *Elementary Textbook of Psychoanalysis,* one of the most widely read books in the field of psychoanalysis, originally published in 1955 and still in print today, grapples with the 13 superstition directly. According to Brenner, Christ's invitation to his disciples to eat bread that was his body and drink wine that was his blood at the Last Supper was the articulation of "a childhood instinctual wish: to kill and devour one's father." The 13-at-a-table superstition arose out of guilt: "Unconsciously, the superstitious Christian ... is telling his father that he is a good son, who does not want to do such a bad thing as to kill and eat him. ... " As for the triskaidekaphobes who have no idea that unlucky 13 originated with the Last Supper, "We may assume . . . that whoever feels strongly about the likelihood that '13' or any other omen will bring him bad luck, is probably unconsciously guilty about something." But not just any something; Brenner adds that a patient's preoccupation with numbers is often a sign of "unconscious preoccupation with masturbation and with the fantasies associated with masturbation."

In 1952, the American Psychiatric Association published the *Diagnostic and Statistical Manual: Mental Disorders* (DSM). It was the first articulation of the general classification system that Coriat and others aspired to in the early years of psychiatry in the United States. DSM was firmly rooted in the psychoanalytic tradition. Someone experiencing a phobia, like triskaidekaphobia, was said to be suffering from a "phobic reaction." This was produced when "a danger signal felt and perceived by the conscious portion of the personality ... becomes detached from a specific idea, object, or situation in daily life and is displaced to some symbolic idea or situation in the form of a specific neurotic fear." In other words, the triskaidekaphobe wasn't afraid of 13 at all; his fear of 13 was just a stand-in for another, more deep-rooted and destructive fear (often involving sex or his mother—or sex with his mother). It was the psychiatrist's job to convince the patient of this, and by convincing him—so the theory goes—cure him. Happily for triskaidekaphobes and Christians alike, psychoanalysis has lost ground as a therapeutic approach over the past half-century.

It is no longer the favored approach to treating mental illness, especially in the case of individuals with significant impairment in social and cognitive functioning.

DIAGNOSIS AND TREATMENT TODAY

Each of the subsequent editions of DSM has moved away from psychoanalysis toward a more empirically based, behavioral approach to the diagnosis of mental disorders. For nearly a decade now, mental-health professionals have relied on the American Psychiatric Association's *Diagnostic and Statistical Manual of Mental Disorders*, Fourth Edition (DSM-IV), to diagnose patients. According to the editorial director of the publishing arm of the APA, it is "the definitive diagnostic and research reference on mental disorders." One diagnosis that does not appear in DSM-IV is triskaidekaphobia. DSM-IV dispenses with the polysyllabic Greek terminology favored by psychoanalysts earlier in the century.

Today, triskaidekaphobia, mysophobia, siderophobia, apeirophobia, and chrematophobia are all subsumed by the diagnosis "specific phobia," and are classified as anxiety disorders, alongside obsessive-compulsive disorder and social phobia. "The essential feature of specific phobia is marked and persistent fear of clearly discernible, circumscribed objects or situations.... The diagnosis is appropriate only if the avoidance, fear, or anxious anticipation of encountering the phobic stimulus interferes significantly with the person's daily routine, occupational functioning, or social life, or if the person is markedly distressed about having the phobia." In other words, most people who believe that

13 is unlucky would not meet today's clinical standard for specific phobia. DSM-IV includes plenty of examples of specific phobias, such as fear of air travel, cats, dogs, snakes, tunnels, bridges, elevators, driving, blood, fainting, dizziness, being shot, heights, closed-in situations, insects, falling, loud sounds—even costumed characters. But not 13. As a specific phobia today, fear of 13 simply does not rate.

In some people today, triskaidekaphobia does, of course, still meet a clinical threshold for phobic disorder, where impairment of cognitive and social functioning necessitates treatment. In this postpsychoanalytic era, the preferred clinical approach to treating phobias is behavior therapy, which uses desensitization—gradual exposure to the object of the phobia—to reduce fear. A triskaidekaphobe who is particularly afraid of the 13th floor might be required to visit the 13th floor of a building and gradually spend more and more time on the floor. This simple treatment approach is remarkably effective and has the advantage of focusing on behavior rather than unverifiable intangibles like the subconscious and infantile sexual fantasies.

TRISKAIDEKAPHOBES, BEWARE

More than most professions, psychiatry is a victim of its past and the media. A constant stream of movies and books have kept alive the fallacy that psychiatry today is synonymous with Freud and psychoanalysis, and that therapy is always about sex and mothers and masturbation. Talk shows and the countless self-help, New Age, and "alternative" books that are published each year offer facile solutions to serious (and imaginary) psychological problems, further confusing the public about the diagnosis and treatment of mental illness. This has allowed "alternative" treatments to exist on a competitive footing with the established, scientific disciplines of psychiatry and psychology. As a result, when triskaidekaphobia becomes serious enough to impede an individual's functioning, or when a mild triskaidekaphobe decides that he wants to rid himself of the phobia and begins to investigate treatment options, he has no idea where to turn. Below are two examples of successful alternative-therapy businesses that specialize in phobias.

"WILL ROGERS WITH A PH.D."

Dr. Donald Dossey has a gift for self-promotion: over the past decade, he has been a frequent guest on TV and radio shows on Friday the 13th, and he is often quoted as an expert on triskaidekaphobia in newspapers and on the Internet. On his Web site, Dr. Dossey poses (and answers) an interesting question:

> Why is Dr. Dossey consistently in the news and interviewed on hundreds of radio and TV talk shows every holiday?

> Because he offers you more than one angle! Many are fascinated by the origins and humorous folklore superstitions of the holidays; others by the numerous phobias and stresses surrounding them. Many prefer both. Dr. Dossey

has appeared on *OPRAH WINFREY*, numerous times on
CNN, *THE OTHER SIDE*, and *HARD COPY*. He is the
Holiday Superstition and Folklore Reporter, and is known
as "the Will Rogers with a Ph.D."

Dr. Dossey is not just a self-proclaimed reporter; he is also
the founder of "the Phobia Institute and the Stress Management
Centers of Southern California and SMC Asheville, North
Carolina." Dr. Dossey uses his Web site and media appearances
to advertise his products and services, including books, audio-
tapes, and telephone consultations aimed at helping people overcome their phobias. The biographical page of Dr. Dossey's Web
site includes the following claims:

> As a behavioral scientist, media personality, and author,
> Dr. Dossey is an internationally acclaimed authority in the
> treatment of anxieties, phobias and stress.... Dr. Dossey
> has created, tested, and adopted a revolutionary new pro-
> gram of telephone consultation which has proven to be
> faster in obtaining results than any other known form of
> one-to-one therapy.

As impressive as the Web page is, it is light on facts. There is
no reference, for example, to the fact that Dr. Dossey's Ph.D. in
psychology is from an obscure distance-learning university
(Heed University of Wisconsin and Florida) that has never been
accredited by the American Psychological Association—the professional standard in the field. Perhaps it is not surprising that he

includes psychotherapy and psychiatry on a list of "controversial treatment modalities" that should be avoided in favor of his own method, contending that "Psychotherapy/psychiatry can be detrimental to mental, emotional and physical health."

Despite his questionable credentials and his wholesale dismissal of an entire scientific discipline, Dr. Dossey has been quoted as an expert on phobias in the following newspapers, magazines, and Web sites, among others: the *Atlanta Journal-Constitution*, the *Austin American-Statesman*, the *Buffalo News*, the *Cincinnati Post*, the *Florida Times Union*, the *Fresno Bee*, the *Morristown Daily Record*, *National Geographic News*, the *Newark Star-Ledger*, *Salon.com*, the *Seattle Times*, *Today's Senior* magazine, and the *Winston-Salem Journal*. The *New York Times* has twice relied on Dr. Dossey as a source, for two very different articles: a 1992 article about a mass murder (in which he was quoted as an expert on posttraumatic stress disorder), and a lighthearted 1997 article in which he offered advice on how to avoid stress during Christmas holiday shopping. Each reference, of course, constitutes an implicit endorsement of Dr. Dossey's services and products, and helps direct triskaidekaphobes to his door.

"FEAR? ANXIETY? PHOBIA?"

The Phobia Clinic is one of a number of alternative therapy services on the Internet that target people with phobias. The "Triskaidekaphobia team" at the Phobia Clinic claims to have great success in treating fear of 13. At the top of the Phobia Clinic's main Web page, visitors are asked in enormous black

letters: "Fear? Anxiety? Phobia?" Directly below is another question: "Will you commit just 24 hours to learn to Live Free of the
Feelings?" I sent the clinic a general query requesting more information. The "Client Administrator" sent back an enthusiastic
e-mail assuring me that the phobia teams don't even need twenty-
four hours to treat phobias: "Here's the bottom line: Pretty well
any Fear or Phobia can be removed in 2–3 hours." Curious about
the clinic's claims, I returned to the site to learn more. I discovered that the Phobia Clinic uses something called "Time Line
Therapy" to treat triskaidekaphobes. According to its Web site:

> Time Line Therapy is a specific process designed to trace a
> particular negative feeling, belief or limiting decision back
> to the first time in memory that it can be found. The theory
> behind this is that problems in the present day are likely to
> have their roots in the past.... The problem could have
> started in childhood, during our birth, whilst we were in
> the womb, from an event in another lifetime or could have
> been something that happened to one of our ancestors.

Time Line Therapy seems to combine psychoanalytic
assumptions about the subconscious and the role the distant past
plays in determining present behavior with New Age concepts
like past-life regression. When I scrolled down to the bottom of
the page, past a faint gray dividing line and an index, I came to a
disclaimer in the same faint gray lettering, which puts the clinic's
claims in proper (and legal) perspective:

> The Phobia Clinic & Change That's Right Now, Inc. and
> the contents of this website have not been evaluated by the
> FDA nor approved by any other government or official
> body. Nothing offered on or offline is intended to diag-
> nose, cure or prevent any disease or disorder of any kind.
> You will not be working with a doctor, psychotherapist,
> psychoanalyst, psychiatrist, psychologist, master of family
> child counseling, or master of social work.

The disclaimer appeared to contradict the confident statement of efficacy made by the client administrator—but it did not
end there. Clicking on a *"More…"* link at the very bottom of the
page brought me to a separate page with a full 1,500-word disclaimer in standard font, above which the clinic offers the following disclaimer on disclaimers: "They are a legal neccessity [*sic*],
but a cop-out, and no substitute for you taking responsibility for
yourself. Therefore we have an important recommendation to
make: *If you really need a disclaimer, this stuff is not for you.*"

I felt as if I had learned all I needed or wanted to learn about
the Phobia Clinic. But the clinic was not yet through with me.
Three months later, I received a mass e-mail from them, which
solicited my participation in a news segment on hydrophobia, the
fear of water. The e-mail emphasized what a great opportunity
this would be to showcase the clinic's (nondiagnostic, noncura-
tive, nonpreventative) approach to phobia removal before a
national audience. Anyone interested in learning more was
invited to reply to "drowningfear03@yahoo.com." As of July
2004, the news segment had not made it on the air, but it would

not have been an anomaly if it had. In early 2004, the Phobia Clinic received extended, positive coverage on an episode of the *Rick Sanchez Show*, which airs on NBC 6 in South Florida.

Triskaidekaphobes, beware. If you are considering treatment for your phobia, there are things it may be unluckier to believe in than unlucky 13.

CHAPTER EIGHT

Triskaidekaphobia Today

When I am reading, I will not stop on page 94, page 193,
page 382, et al.—the digits of these numbers add up to 13.

—Stephen King

I N 2000, A SURVEY of ten popular superstitions in *American
Demographics* magazine found that exactly 13 percent of
Americans believe that Friday the 13th is unlucky. Among 18- to
24-year-olds, that number jumped to 30 percent. Although this is
a sizable percentage, it is a far cry from the percentage of believers
during triskaidekaphobia's heyday. Back in 1933, a study of college
students found that over 90 percent believed Friday the 13th was
unlucky. In 2000, Friday the 13th ranked behind walking under a
ladder, breaking a mirror, and having one's path crossed by a
black cat. Clearly, Friday the 13th has seen better days. It is, how-

ever, the last unlucky 13 superstition to afflict a significant percentage of the population—which explains why the survey did not even list any of the other 13 superstitions. At the start of the twenty-first century, unlucky 13 is well on its way to becoming unlucky Friday the 13th.

If a superstition being accommodated by businesses is a good indication of its vitality, then Friday the 13th still has teeth today. When Texas Instruments offered an early retirement plan recently, employees asked why the official retirement date was on a Monday instead of a Friday (as tradition dictates). The human resources department explained that the previous Friday was Friday the 13th and they did not want that to be employees' official retirement date. Although its influence is no longer what it once was, Friday the 13th continues to impact the economy. Park rangers report that groups avoid planning trips to state parks on the date. According to travel agents, people still avoid flying on Friday the 13th. Die-hard triskaidekaphobes do not stop with air travel; they will avoid scheduling meetings, interviews, tests, and dentist appointments on that day. Even among people who otherwise pay no attention to 13, Friday the 13th still has enough of a presence in our culture that some people joke about it when it arrives and others breathe a sigh of relief when it is gone.

In fact, a number of recent studies suggest that Friday the 13th is actually dangerous. There has been a consistent finding that more traffic accidents and traffic fatalities occur on Friday the 13th than on other days of the year. A 2002 study in the United Kingdom found that hospital admissions "due to transport accidents were significantly increased on Friday the 13th." The study concluded that the "risk of hospital admission as a result of a transport accident may be increased by as much as 52 percent," and ended with the following advice: "Staying at home is recommended." In 2001, a study in Finland of traffic deaths on Friday the 13th between 1971 and 1997 found that it was more dangerous than other days of the year specifically for female drivers: "the risk of death for women who venture into traffic on this unlucky day is higher by 63 percent." A century ago, these studies would have been interpreted as damning evidence that 13 was a real and malevolent force in the world, and could conceivably have influenced the course of the superstition in the twentieth century. One hundred years later, researchers arrived at a different conclusion: never wavering from the assumption that Friday the 13th is not objectively unlucky, they concluded that the anxiety some people feel about the day is enough to make it a self-fulfilling prophecy.

THE QUESTIONNAIRE

Superstition has always been primarily an oral tradition. In order to learn what people had to say about unlucky 13 today, over a nine-month period in 2003 I distributed a completely unscientific questionnaire via the Internet. I received close to a thousand replies. It is, of course, difficult to assess the prevalence of a superstition in a culture that views superstitions as sinful, ignorant, irrational, destructive, and ludicrous; many mild to moderate triskaidekaphobes hide their beliefs to keep the smirks and scorn to a minimum. Nonetheless, people on every side of 13— triskaidekaphobes, triskaidekaphiles, and those who view 13 as just a number—consistently reported that, while they believed unlucky 13 was one of our most popular superstitions, they did not think it was as prevalent as it used to be. There was a wide range of theories about its origin. Where a century ago almost everyone would have agreed that it originated with the Last Supper, today there is very little consensus. The various alternative theories were mentioned more often than the Last Supper, and only a few respondents had heard of unlucky 13 at a table.

Very few triskaidekaphobes today connect unlucky 13 to the Last Supper. Even fewer list it as the reason *they* believe the number is unlucky. Most do not have a theory about unlucky 13's origin. They don't need one: Their belief comes from their own experiences, and they assume that this is the way it has always been. A forty-four-year-old social worker from Indiana, for example, traces her fear of 13 to an adolescent experiment: one Friday the 13th she and a friend placed a tape recorder in a graveyard overnight to see if they could "pick up sounds from beyond the grave." She remembers, "We did get some sounds that seemed incredible for such a low-tech machine and one sound in particular that could not be explained and bothered us." Fear of 13 has dogged her ever since. A year ago she moved into an apartment numbered 4113, and now wonders whether the address might be to blame for her family's recent financial difficulties.

The development of triskaidekaphobia often follows a similar pattern: awareness of the phenomenon of unlucky 13 leads to increased sensitivity to the number, which, helped along by a negative 13 experience or two, results in full-blown triskaidekaphobia. Thus a forty-year-old man from Wisconsin attributes his "paranoia" about Friday the 13th to the unexpected death of his grandmother on that date. His belief has intensified over the years because his dog had to be put to sleep on a Friday the 13th and a family friend fell off a roof and broke his back on the 13th of the month. Once a triskaidekaphobe accepts the idea that 13 is unlucky, it is not hard to find confirmation—especially if one discounts the good things that happen on the 13th and the bad things that happen on other days.

Today, the experiential approach to 13 dominates. Most people who believe in unlucky 13 will, when called upon to defend themselves, describe their unlucky experiences with the number. Similarly, most people who reject the superstition, if asked why, will say that they have not had any bad experiences with the number. This idea would have been completely foreign to nineteenth- and early-twentieth-century triskaidekaphobes. Back then, personal experience didn't come into it. People *knew* that 13 was unlucky, and why—the Last Supper—and did whatever they could to avoid its malign influence. A person could live his entire life without being visited by 13's bad luck and still believe it was unlucky—and find nothing strange in that. Triskaidekaphobia drew strength from its association with the Last Supper. With that connection lost and the proliferation of so many competing theories about 13's origin, triskaidekaphobia has nothing but individual experience to feed on—that and public awareness of the superstition's existence.

THE MEDIA

In an era in which fewer and fewer people believe in unlucky 13, the superstition's survival is more dependent on the media than ever before. The role of the media in sustaining unlucky 13, especially Friday the 13th, cannot be overestimated. Many people take notice of Friday the 13th only because it is featured in newspapers and on TV and the radio. A number of mild triskaidekaphobes reported that they sometimes forget the date until they turn on the TV or radio and are reminded that they should be frightened.

A good example of the media's influence on unlucky 13 is the recent A&E documentary *Superstitions: Unlucky 13*, an episode of *The Unexplained*, an ongoing series. One of the few documentaries to examine unlucky 13 at any length, *Superstitions* portrays itself as a serious investigation of the validity of the superstition and a comprehensive examination of its origins. But like many TV documentaries that purport to bring history to life, A&E's treatment of 13 is haphazard, misleading, and inaccurate. The first two-thirds of the forty-five-minute program is devoted to two wildly disparate events: the ill-fated *Apollo 13* lunar mission in 1970, and the suicide of Ray Johnson, an offbeat Manhattan artist, on Friday, January 13, 1995. The opening narration implies that the film is going to use the events as case studies to explore whether or not unlucky 13 has any basis in fact.

Ever since the explosion on *Apollo 13* on April 13, 1970, which ended NASA's third lunar landing mission prematurely and almost resulted in the death of the three-man crew, triskaidekaphobes have speculated that the number played a role in its fate. In addition to the mission's name and the fact that the explosion took place on April 13th, triskaidekaphobes point out three other 13s: *Apollo 13* left launchpad 39 (13 x 3) at 1313 hours on 4/11/70 (the digits of which add up to 13). Usually left out of the discussion are all the other numbers that had nothing to do with 13. For example, main booster engine 5 shut down shortly after liftoff and the explosion, which took place on the third day of the mission at 2107 hours, occurred in oxygen tank 2, etc....

The *Apollo 13* section of *Superstitions* includes interviews with Jim Lovell, the mission's commander, and an astronomer, both of whom reject the notion that unlucky 13 played a role, and an astrologer, who argues that the *stars* played a role but is vague about 13. The section includes a wealth of visuals from old news reports, most of which have nothing to do with unlucky 13 but add ready-made production value to the documentary.

The Ray Johnson section uses interviews with the artist's friends and colleagues and a plethora of ridiculous camera angles, reenactments (we see something splash into the water where he drowned umpteen times), and canned suspense music to explore whether or not he killed himself on Friday the 13th intentionally, and, if he did, what kind of artistic statement he might have been making. If the emphasis on *Apollo 13* is myopic, the time devoted to Johnson's suicide is gratuitously macabre and bewildering in its irrelevance. Whether or not he cared that it was Friday the 13th says nothing about the validity of the superstition. The sole purpose of this section seems to be an appeal to the audience's insatiable appetite for true crime.

The last third of *Superstitions* is a hodgepodge of speculation and trivia about the origin and history of unlucky 13. This section highlights two of the most popular alternative theories: the death of Baldur in Norse mythology and Christianity's attempt to stifle paganism. But the narrator sums up the question of the origin of 13 as follows: "Is the notion of unlucky 13 simply a throwback to so-called pagan beliefs from over three thousand years ago, or is it a curse which has been passed down to us based on an ancient mystery that remains unexplained?" The audience is left in the dark about what the curse or ancient mystery might be and why the producers think this is the most likely alternative to three-thousand-year-old pagan beliefs—but the question does manage to neatly echo the title of the series, *The Unexplained.*

Despite its many failings, *Superstitions* was identified by dozens of people who answered the questionnaire as the source that has most influenced their view of unlucky 13. Given how few books and documentaries have examined the superstition, and given that millions of people saw *Superstitions* in its initial airing (and in its rebroadcasts since), it is entirely conceivable that it has permanently changed the public's understanding of the importance of *Apollo 13* in the history and lore of unlucky 13, and transformed a recent suicide of a little-known artist into a significant event in the history of the world's most popular superstition.

OTHER UNLUCKY NUMBERS

Even in its heyday, 13 was not the only unlucky number in our culture. There was always the *other* unlucky biblical number:

REVELATION (13:18): Let him that hath understanding count the number of the beast: for it is the number of a man; and his number Six hundred threescore and six.

I received dozens of questionnaires from people who think 13 is nothing compared to 666—who hold their heads high on Friday the 13th and have no problem with the 13th floor, but would never accept a credit card with 666 in it or visit the Isamu Noguchi Garden Museum at 666 Fifth Avenue in Manhattan or stay at the Econolodge at 666 North Wells Avenue in Reno, Nevada. The World Financial Network National Bank, which underwrites private-label credit cards for major retailers, has seen evidence that 666 holds more sway than 13. According to a customer service employee: "Anything involving 666 seems to get some people into a frenzy. When one of our client's cards reached the series starting with 666, we got a ton of them back and a bunch of frantic calls from people wanting a new account number."

Another popular number superstition has survived into the twenty-first century despite—rather than because of—its biblical associations. The number three's positive association with the Holy Trinity has not kept the belief that bad things come in threes from being popular. As with most superstitions, this one has several variations. Besides the general formulation, there is the superstition that any bad deed will be returned three times over—many Wiccans use this as motivation to practice only good magic—and the even more popular superstition that death comes in threes, especially celebrity deaths.

In addition to shared number superstitions like 13, 666, and bad things coming in 3s, many people have their own individual number superstitions. Although the belief in lucky numbers seems to be more common than the belief in unlucky numbers (13 excepted), for any number under 100, there is someone, somewhere, who thinks of it as his unlucky number. The reasons vary. Sometimes there aren't even reasons; sometimes a person simply has a "bad feeling" about a number and will avoid it the rest of his life. One fairly common unlucky number superstition is the belief that one will die at a certain age. A thirty-four-year-old assistant professor from Minneapolis told me that he worries he will die at fifty-one because that was the age at which his father died. A World War II veteran who was assigned the number fifty-seven in his regiment and was shot in the head at the battle of Arnhem was convinced that he would die at fifty-seven—until he made it to fifty-eight. As in the case of 13, in some people this belief can escalate to the point where it becomes debilitating, especially as the number closes in.

Most people today seem to be aware that triskaidekaphobia's hold over us is not what it once was. Whether or not they know anything about the superstition's history, there is the intuitive sense that its best days are behind it. Not even the persistent phenomenon of the missing 13th floor or the media coverage every Friday the 13th is enough to disguise its dissipation. The Thirteen Club was right to think that unlucky 13 was not invulnerable to attack. But whether they were right to think that dethroning the world's most popular superstition would undermine superstition's place in our lives is something else entirely.

CHAPTER NINE

Triskaidekaphilia Today

There is a superstition in avoiding superstition, when men think to do best if they go furthest from the superstition formerly received.

—Francis Bacon, *The Essays or Counsels Civil and Moral of Francis Bacon* (1625)

T HE THIRTEEN CLUBBERS of the late nineteenth century would have been thrilled with the declining status of triskaidekaphobia today. But they would have been considerably less enthusiastic about the fact that another 13 superstition—triskaidekaphilia—has emerged as the driving force behind efforts to kill off unlucky 13. Not since the Thirteen Club's campaign peaked in the 1890s has unlucky 13 experienced such a sustained attack. Contemporary triskaidekaphiles fall into three camps: people who have been exposed to a positive 13 in their own lives (e.g., a birthday or anniversary on the 13th), contrarians who favor 13 because they like the idea of flouting the unlucky 13 superstition, and the growing contingent of devotees to esoteric belief systems that claim 13 has been misunderstood and is really a benevolent, mystical number. One trait shared by all triskaidekaphiles is the fact that their belief in lucky 13 is dependent on the existence of triskaidekaphobia. If unlucky 13 had never been popular, the phenomenon of triskaidekaphilia would not exist today.

Ironically, as triskaidekaphobia fades, the popular idea that most people believe in unlucky 13 is fueling the rise of triskaidekaphilia. In a culture in which awareness of the popularity of unlucky 13 greatly exceeds actual belief in it, flouting the superstition gives people the satisfaction of rejecting something many are supposed to believe, with little risk of incurring stigma from triskaidekaphobes. Triskaidekaphilia has even gone commercial. Dozens of companies manufacture products—charms, rings, belt buckles, decals, etc.—that prominently display 13 on them for the growing numbers of triskaidekaphiles among us. *Lucky 13* itself has become a catchphrase, featured on T-shirts, hats, even baby clothes, thanks to companies like Lucky Brand Dungarees and Lucky 13 Apparel (slogan: "Lucky 13 . . . not just a name, but a lifestyle!"), which sell clothes and other items emblazoned with the once-improbable phrase.

13 EXPOSURE

In these post-triskaidekaphobic days, people born on the 13th are more likely than anyone else to become triskaidekaphiles. The superstition is no longer strong enough—usually—for them to

MUSICAL 13

1
"13 Club Galop" (1885)
—John K. Conner

2
"13 I'm So Unlucky 13" (1922)
—Joseph Samuels Jazz Band

3
"Unlucky 13 Blues" (1939)
—Roosevelt Sykes

4
"Born on the 13th" (1952)
—Willie Smokey Hogg

5
"Friday the 13th" (1953)
—Thelonious Monk

6
"Thirteen" (1961)
—Eric Dolphy

7

"Thirteen Highway" (1963)

—Muddy Waters

8

"Lucky Thirteen" (1965)

—Bert Jansch

9

"Friday the 13th Child" (1973)

—Bobby Bland

10

"13th House" (1981)

—McCoy Tyner

11

"Thirteen Steps Lead Down" (1994)

—Elvis Costello

12

"Thirteen" (1999)

—Danzig

13

"Lucky 13 Blues" (2000)

—Brother Yusef

condemn themselves as unlucky, but it is still well known enough that they often reject it by claiming 13 as their lucky number. A real estate broker from Hawaii who was born on Friday the 13th characterizes this perspective as "counter-phobic." Although she does not really believe that 13 is objectively lucky, she takes a stand against unlucky 13 by claiming it as her lucky number—a strategy pioneered by the Thirteen Club. A twenty-three-year-old massage therapist from Dallas born on February 13 has believed that 13 is her lucky number for as long as she can remember. She chose number 13 when she played sports in high school, and today she bets on 13 when she gambles. "I find it a liberating number," she explains, "one that goes against the grain. I always feel special and unique when I tell someone my favorite number is 13." There is something undeniably appealing about rejecting something other people fear. The appeal is so great for some triskaidekaphiles that they resort to creative numerology to bring lucky 13 into their birthdays. A forty-three-year-old neopagan who calls herself Aradia GoldenDove believes 13 is her lucky number and Friday the 13th is her lucky day because "I was born on the 31st of the month. As you can see, 31 is 13 reversed."

Back when triskaidekaphobia was king, having a birthday on the 13th was one of the few lucky exceptions to the superstition: if you were born on the 13th, 13 was your lucky number. This exception probably developed as an escape clause. It would have been especially cruel to condemn someone to lifelong bad luck because of the date on which he happened to be born. But not everyone at the time accepted the lucky exception to unlucky 13. There was also a superstition in circulation that it *was* unlucky to be born on the 13th. Various terrible fates were predicted—a short life, a life filled with bad luck—but usually the afflicted was offered a corollary that softened the blow. The bad luck would be lessened if parents concealed their child's birth date, and it would stop when the last person who knew the true date died.

By exposing their families to their triskaidekaphilia, people born on the 13th inspire new generations of triskaidekaphiles. A forty-nine-year-old nurse practitioner from Florida whose father was born on the 13th and was the 13th child in his family explained that he was raised to believe that 13 was "a good and positive number," and to challenge triskaidekaphobia on all fronts. His take on 13 today? "For me it is a lucky number. If everyone avoids the number 13, think how much good luck is left for those who don't!" Sometimes all it takes is one or two dedicated triskaidekaphiles to create a clan of like-minded family members. One loyal and enthusiastic husband declares: "I'm not triskaidekaphobic! In fact, we consider Friday the 13th to be a lucky day at my house. My wife was born on Friday the 13th." In another family the parents met on a ship on July 13th. It was love at first sight; today, everyone in the family wishes them "Happy 13th" on their anniversary and whenever Friday the 13th rolls around. Family triskaidekaphilia is often strong enough to withstand evidence that 13 is not always lucky. A twenty-one-year-old body piercer in Denver reports that she inherited her love of 13 from her father, who was born on the 13th. They even named a stray black cat they used to feed Thirteen. One Christmas Eve a few years ago, Thirteen chewed through the Christmas lights on their porch and was electrocuted. The experience has not changed their belief in lucky 13.

Today, more than ever before, a positive 13 experience has the potential to turn a person who was indifferent to the number into a lifelong triskaidekaphile. A forty-eight-year-old journalist from New Jersey told me that 13 has been her lucky number since she was assigned it at her first job, as a waitress in an ice cream parlor, twenty-two years ago. In a speech at the National Press Club on Friday, September 13, 2002, General Richard B. Myers, chairman of the Joint Chiefs of Staff, told a roomful of journalists that 13 had been his lucky number since he was a fighter pilot in Vietnam. "I flew with the 13th Tactical Fighter Squadron. And the peg that I used to hang my life-support equipment, my helmet, my G-suit, and so forth on was peg 13. So if I can survive getting shot at and hanging around the number 13, I figured that showing up at the National Press Club on Friday the 13th shouldn't be all that big a threat."

Many triskaidekaphiles are first exposed to 13 through sports. Athletes who are assigned jersey 13 often wind up considering it their lucky number. Beth Bass, CEO of the Women's Basketball Coaches Association, was forced to wear 13 when she played for the Fighting Red Foxes of Hartsville High in Hartsville, South Carolina, because it was the only jersey available. Ever since, she has had a deep affinity for 13. A high-school volleyball coach in Michigan wrote that 13 has been her lucky number since winning her first trophy in track, wearing number 713, back in 1972. She reported that 13 has never been turned down on her volleyball squads, and speculated that "the old superstitions do not have the meaning they used to."

There is at least one example of institutionalized triskaidekaphilia in the United States, which exposes hundreds of young people to lucky 13 every year. Colgate University may well be the only institution in the world that formally sides itself with 13. When its president, Rebecca Chopp, addressed the new freshman class in the fall of 2002, she informed the uninitiated, "For Colgaters, 13 is lucky.... We love 13." According to the university's Web site, this unique academic tradition dates back to the early beginnings of the school: "The University developed from the Baptist Education Society of the State of New York, which was founded in 1819 by '13 men with 13 dollars, 13 prayers, and 13 articles'—hence the lucky-13 tradition at Colgate." During the convocation ceremony, President Chopp had harsh words for triskaidekaphobes. "Why do we ban triskaidekaphobia at Colgate? Because we are dedicated to not being superstitious, not being conformist, not staying comfortable in our little boxes, not putting people in stereotypes." After entreating the class of 2006 to say the word *triskaidekaphobia* with her, President Chopp informed them: "On Colgate's campus, it is forbidden.... One more time, say it with me: *Triskaidekaphobia*. It is forbidden!" Had there been any triskaidekaphobes in the audience, they might have questioned the demand for conformity and the stereotyping of the superstitious. But that seems unlikely—the guides on campus tours for prospective freshmen at Colgate are just as vocal about triskaidekaphobia as the president is during convocation ceremonies.

CONTRARIANS

Contrarian triskaidekaphiles have been around since the days of the Thirteen Club. They call 13 lucky to scorn the superstition.

This worked better when unlucky 13 was more vital and pervasive, and some triskaidekaphiles are nostalgic for the old days. "I always liked Friday the 13th when I was growing up," one triskaidekaphile explained. "So many people were walking around spooked about it that it gave the rest of us the opportunity to look daring by letting black cats cross our paths or by stepping on cracks in the sidewalk." One colorful subcategory of contrarian triskaidekaphile isn't really about 13 as much as it is about romanticizing 13's association with death. These are the Goth types who like wearing black, 13 charms, and skull jewelry, who rebel by flirting with what most of us ignore or fear. Most aren't aware of the mortal 13-at-a-table superstition, and instead draw upon the association of 13 with the devil and witchcraft, or the Death card in Tarot.

Another popular contrarian belief is that Friday the 13th is a good day for gambling. According to a professional blackjack dealer in Las Vegas, the superstition is no superstition: "If you want better odds in Vegas, Friday the 13th is always good for the player and costly for the house. I don't know why it is, but I've seen it happen for a while now." In light of this perspective, it is not surprising that there is an established tradition among gamblers of planning trips to Las Vegas around Friday the 13th. But when it comes to gambling, lucky 13 is not limited to Las Vegas or Friday the 13th. As one frequent gambler put it, "Thirteen is a number to play, and a date to play on, everywhere." The tradition of betting on 13 is an old and honorable one. A 1903 *New York Times* article headlined the "Origin of Common Superstitions" observed: "How inconsistent men are! Go to a raffle or to a lottery, and notice how anxious everybody is to secure the number

13. It is about the first number that a person who has a choice will take." Today, a number of states, including Colorado, Connecticut, Kentucky, and New Hampshire, have "Lucky 13" scratch-off instant lottery games. However, there are exceptions to the gambler's lucky 13. As several Vegas locals report, "You will never find a 13th floor in any high-rise here." Even in the gambling capital of the world, not every 13 is considered lucky.

VICTIMIZED 13

Unlike the 13 superstition itself, neopagan beliefs do not represent a historically continuous, integrated cultural tradition. This has not stopped proponents from drawing much of their authority from claims to the contrary. It is no small irony that Margaret Murray's discredited theory that the witch trials were a Christian attempt to destroy seventeenth-century paganism has helped spawn a neopagan movement based on the false belief that Christianity is its age-old nemesis. Neopagans embrace 13 as a poorly treated, misunderstood, mystical number with history on its side; in other words, they see 13 much the way they see themselves. Many, especially feminist-Wiccans, believe that Friday the 13th is an unusually good and potent day because of the "double power" of Friday and 13. Friday was the day of Freya, the Norse goddess of fertility, and 13 represents the lunar-menstrual-goddess cycle, making Friday the 13th "an incredibly powerful day to conduct any spells or rituals regarding friendships, love, and good luck in general," according to a twenty-eight-year-old sales assistant from New Zealand, whose "witch name" is

Diamond Tiger. A New York City police dispatcher whose department's call sign is 13 and who describes herself as "an Isian witch" says that she thinks of Friday the 13th as a pagan holiday—an antidote to Christmas.

Most neopagans view 13 as a benevolent force; some, with the following caveat: Because it is the believer who instills a number with negative or positive power, 13 is lucky only if you believe it is. A fifteen-year-old neopagan from California explained the idea: "Those who find 13 unlucky will most likely get a return on the power they give it, from simple mistakes to all-out disasters. For those who find it magically positive or even 'sacred,' only beneficial powers are likely to be returned." Not a few people who share this view seem to enjoy the idea that people who believe 13 is unlucky make it unlucky just for themselves; they see the phenomenon of unlucky 13 as evidence of the precept that you become what you believe. Others believe that only bad can come from so many people fearing 13. A twenty-two-year-old cashier from Los Angeles explained: "For those people that hold fear in the number 13, they will project all that is unconscious in them and it will live and have an effect outside themselves and become real. If everyone does this we have a 'collective' problem number. Due to the effect of suggestion on the human mind it then takes people who go out of their way to show that the number 13 has no affect on them to counteract the negative views of 13."

The influence of neopaganism on triskaidekaphobia is growing. Thanks to the Internet, neopaganism is reaching people at younger and younger ages, undermining unlucky 13 before it has a chance to take root. A fifteen-year-old girl from northern California reversed her perspective on Friday the 13th between the age of twelve and fourteen, when she first embraced paganism. Back in her "childhood," she and her friends "would unconsciously try to look for omens of bad luck on Friday the 13th, like finding a plastic bottle pointing at you or seeing a stray cat run across the field. Now, I look forward to when the 13th falls upon a Friday. I look upon it as a great love spell day. The vibes of mystery abound, everyone opening their minds to the pangs of Magick."

Many neopagans see 13 as a victim of the same forces that, they are convinced, oppressed their ancestors. According to an Internet Wiccan from Pennsylvania, "Wiccan wise ones who refused to give up the worship of the lunar goddess were burned at the stake for witchcraft. It's truly a sad history, destroying the natural spirit of people to become slaves for the profitable. Thirteen helped me face the truth and follow the natural spirit of nature." A forty-nine-year-old psychic reader from Baltimore puts the matter more forcefully: "I have learned that all of the ways we count time is a lie. The system of twelve is a lie. If you count time by the perfect 28-day cycle you will find one month has two full moons. Therefore we are not on a system of twelve, we are on a system of thirteen. Unlucky thirteen is a control drama and a way to keep us from 'knowing.'" For every neopagan who views 13 as a misunderstood, benevolent number, there are at least a coven's worth who see more sinister forces at work.

CHAPTER TEN

Conspiratorial 13

The McDonald's symbol is really a 13.

—Internet rumor

WITH THE ARRIVAL of the Internet, conspiracy theorists have found the perfect medium for the dissemination of their beliefs. Conspiracy theories about unlucky 13 have been particularly successful online because there is so much confusion about the superstition's origins, so few real-world resources that treat it at any length, and such a great (and growing) disparity between the number of people who are aware of the superstition and the number of people who actually subscribe to it. Even an informal survey of how people look at unlucky 13 today reveals the plethora of ad hoc and often truly outlandish beliefs that have coalesced around the number. Inasmuch as they are

irrational beliefs motivated by fear, they qualify as a new generation of superstitions about 13. Inasmuch as they involve sinister
and secret plots to control the thoughts and actions of
triskaidekaphobes, they qualify as conspiracy theories. They are
all products of the past fifty years, invented after the fear of 13 had
peaked. Most are inspired by neopaganism and involve a belief in
triskaidekaphilia. Their proponents put more stress on 13's mystical properties than triskaidekaphobes ever have on its bad luck or
the Church ever has on its sinfulness. You will never encounter a
triskaidekaphobe who believes that any of these ideas is the true
origin of unlucky 13; these theories are always about why *other
people* make the mistake of believing in unlucky 13.

THE CHRISTIAN CONSPIRACY

The most popular 13 conspiracy is the belief that unlucky 13 was
created by the Catholic Church in a calculated attempt to kill
off pagan religions that viewed 13 as a benevolent and mystical
number. The popularity of this theory is surprising, not only
because it contradicts all known facts, but also because the
Church remains vocal today about its rejection of superstitions
like 13—a fact that many neopagans must be aware of, since
many of them are former Christians. Ironically, neopagans and
their self-proclaimed nemesis, the Church, both believe that 13
is a benevolent number and that triskaidekaphobia should be
eradicated. The key difference between them is that while
Catholics are taught to view the superstitious as ignorant and
modestly sinful, neopagans are offered an even more seductive

and self-aggrandizing perspective: the superstitious have been duped or, better yet, co-opted by a malevolent ideology bent on their spiritual destruction.

The characteristics of the pagan religion that the Church was supposed to have targeted by promoting triskaidekaphobia vary depending on whom one asks; neopaganism is nothing if not eclectic. Succeeding generations have adapted Margaret Murray's thesis about the witch cult and Gerald Gardner's descriptions of its rites to suit their own interests. One of the more inventive and self-aggrandizing theories is that Jesus Christ was really the most famous and misunderstood witch in history—the leader of a powerful coven made up of himself and the twelve disciples. This idea is gaining popularity thanks to the Internet. Contemporary feminists who embrace neopaganism tend to infuse the conspiracy with feminist ideology: Murray's witch cult was a goddess religion that honored the 13-month lunar cycle. By making the public believe that 13 was unlucky, patriarchal Christianity was attempting to subjugate the power and independence of women. Many respondents to my questionnaire voiced this point of view. A forty-seven-year-old neopagan moon-worshipper from Iowa wrote: "Thirteen is a holy number because of the moon and menstrual cycles. It always has been, but this fact has been suppressed by Church propaganda." A Wiccan college student from the United Kingdom reported an interesting twist: "I have heard that 13 is only unlucky for men. Men tried to demonize Friday the 13th because there are 13 new moons in a year, and Friday is named after the Goddess Freya—double female energy. But they only made it unlucky for themselves."

Of all the conspiracy theorists, the feminist neopagan contingent is the most dedicated. Inflamed by a potent mix of radical feminism and mysticism, they see reclaiming unlucky 13 as a mission of revolutionary significance—one of the great social injustices that still needs to be redressed. One Wiccan yoga instructor who has written extensively on the importance of women "honoring their belly as the dwelling place of the Sacred Feminine" has also devoted considerable energy to combating the 13 superstition. Like many Wiccans, she enthusiastically subscribes to the belief that unlucky 13 is a result of the historical and contemporary subjugation of women: "I have strong feelings about the number 13 as it relates to the cultural history (and suppression) of women and the conscious feminine in patriarchal society. The number 13 evokes fear because of culturally imposed ignorance and prejudice. I feel that it's important to dispel the fear that separates and subordinates us in relation to each other."

Other proponents of the Christian conspiracy theory couch the same beliefs in more abstract New Age terminology. A fifty-seven-year-old self-described "Artisan/Honorary Scholar—Cadre 1/Entity 7" from Arizona claims, "The number (energy) of 13 is actually an important KEY to the 'NEW AGE' or shift of consciousness which is now coming into manifestation." When I asked her to elaborate on this important KEY, she explained:

> We have been living in an "artificially created" closed system of twelves. There are actually 13 lunar cycles in the year, but the Gregorian calendar imposed a 12-month system on us, which distorts our ability to live in harmony

with natural rhythms and cycles of nature and time. Twelve is stable; that is why it was imposed on the calendar by the Church, which was the political power at the time, in order to keep the populace under control.

The theory that the shift to the Gregorian calendar was motivated by a desire to suppress a natural and mystical "13 force" has many variations; what they all have in common is the belief that the transition from the lunar to the solar calendar was a calculated effort by the Church to destroy our primordial connection to nature. In fact, many neopagans advocate a return to a lunar calendar system. One New Age contingent has attempted to revive the Mayan calendar; Web sites extol the special powers its contemporary followers enjoy, including enhanced telepathy, synchronicity, and intelligence. Regardless of the specific characteristics of the "oppressed" belief system, most contemporary 13 conspiracy theories view the Church as their oppressor. In the few cases where the Church is not the culprit, it is that old standby, "the government."

THE KNIGHTS TEMPLAR, JASON VOORHEES, AND THE ONE-DOLLAR BILL

In the twentieth century, more than six hundred years after their demise, the Knights Templar became a lightning rod for an array of bewildering beliefs: They were the possessors of the Holy Grail and/or the Ark of the Covenant; Christ, Christopher Columbus, George Washington, and a host of other historical figures who lived and died either long before or long after the Templars were actually active, secret members of the order; the Templars escaped the trap set by France's King Philip IV and survive to this day.... Another popular belief about the Templars is that they harnessed the mystical power of 13; that is how they became so wealthy and such a threat to the established order. In fact, one of the most widely circulated conspiracy theories is that King Philip IV and Pope Clement V planned the Templars' mass arrest for Friday the 13th just to inspire the belief that 13 was unlucky, thereby reducing the likelihood that others would uncover the potency of 13. Templar-related conspiracy theories are especially popular among neopagans and New Agers, many of whom identify with the Knights Templar as another persecuted, misunderstood, mystical society whose aim was to help the world become a better place. Some even claim to be lineal descendants of this famous order.

Ironically, one proponent of the 13–Knights Templar conspiracy theory is former child actor Ari Lehman, who in 1980 starred in the original *Friday the 13th*. Lehman played Jason Voorhees, the drowned son of Mrs. Voorhees, who terrorizes Camp Crystal Lake to avenge his death. Lehman appears on-screen for less than fifteen seconds—first, in Mrs. Voorhees's memories, then in a brief but terrifying dream sequence. After beheading Mrs. Voorhees, Alice, the last counselor left alive at Camp Crystal Lake, rows a boat out onto the lake and waits for the police. She wakes up at dawn, just as the police arrive. Suddenly, Jason, decomposing and covered in muck, jumps out of the water and pulls her under. Alice wakes up from her nightmare in a hospital bed. When she learns that no boy was found among the bodies at the camp, she faces the camera with unfocused eyes and utters the film's eerie closing line: "Then, he's still out there." This brief dream sequence is one of the scarier moments in movie history and has helped make Jason one of the most famous horror icons of all time.

While making *Friday the 13th*, the fourteen-year-old Lehman thought a great deal about the date and why it was singled out as significant. Nearly a quarter century later, Lehman, now a professional musician, still feels the impact of his most memorable film role. In his reply to my questionnaire on 13, he explained, "My curiosity about 13 has led me on a path of esoteric discovery that I still pursue to this day." A confirmed triskaidekaphile, Lehman believes that the Knights Templar, the Freemasons, and many of the founding fathers were all members of a secret sect that drew its power from the number 13. Thirteen "protects those who revere it, like some sort of mystical talisman." The proof, Lehman contends, is all those 13s on the back of the one-dollar bill—13 steps on the pyramid, 13 letters in *Annuit Coeptis*, 13 plumes of feathers on each of the eagle's wings, 13 bars on the shield, 13 leaves on the olive branch, 13 arrows, 13 stars, and 13 letters in *E Pluribus Unum*. "Anyone who tells you it is all because of the original 13 colonies is missing the big picture. Why did our founding fathers wait until there were 13 colonies to declare independence from the British crown, in a year that also represented 13 to them, the 76th year of the 1700s, 1776, when $7 + 6 = 13$. Another coincidence? Not likely."

Lehman believes that the United States has benefited from the protection of 13 throughout its history and that the sect survives to this day. In his view the unlucky 13 superstition is a smoke-screen designed to obscure the power of 13. Like many conspiracy theorists, Lehman sees triskaidekaphilia as a calling—a message the world needs to hear. Lucky 13 is an untapped resource that, once recognized, can and will change the world, one triskaideka-phile at a time. According to Lehman: "The discovery of 13 has an empowering and liberating effect on the mind and soul, by affirm-ing that every abstract entity is multifaceted, not monolithic, and that archaic societal prejudices, once properly challenged, quickly fall apart to reveal deeper and more universal truths underlying the false veneer of consensual deception."

The alleged connection between the mystical powers of 13 and the founding fathers is not Lehman's invention. With or without the link to the Knights Templar, it is a popular 13 conspir-acy in its own right—one that has received considerable exposure on the Internet and in the real world. The best-selling books of astrologer Linda Goodman—according to one of her publishers, her books have sold more than 60 million copies—make similar claims. In *Star Signs*, she analyzes the patterns of 13 on the dollar bill. She interprets the pyramid design on the bill as evidence of the founding fathers' mystical connection to ancient Egyptian beliefs, and Congress's failed efforts to remove it as unsuccessful attempts by the "dark forces on Earth" to undermine the protec-tion it afforded our nation. The fact that Congress never suc-ceeded is evidence of "Divine protection." Like many New Agers, Goodman holds 13 in high regard, ascribing more power to it than any triskaidekaphobe ever has: "Thirteen is not an unlucky num-ber, as many people believe. The ancients claimed that 'he who understands how to use the number 13 will be given power and dominion.' " Although she neglects to explain which "ancients" she is referring to, it *does* sound like the way ancients would talk.

MISCELLANY

People who believe that 13 is the victim of a coordinated conspiracy stretching across centuries (or millennia) are passionate and dedicated, and they want change. No matter who is painted as the villain, conspiracy theorists invariably view the 13 superstition as a coordinated effort to keep the magic and power of benevolent 13 from the masses. In their own minds, their triskaidekaphilia marks them as the descendants of a select group of extraordinary individuals—whether mystical pagans or the Knights Templar— and heirs to an important secret: the power of 13. Conspiratorial 13 gives them an identity, a sense of purpose, and the intoxicating feeling that they stand apart from the unenlightened masses. For every proponent of one of the theories above, there is another triskaidekaphile who takes conspiratorial 13 and adapts it to suit his own interests and inclinations. The democracy of the Internet is fertile ground for other fringe theories involving 13. One fifty-four-year-old Canadian responded to my questionnaire by pitching his Internet-based triskaidekaphile business. Invoking the Mayan lunar calendar, it revolves around a mystical "Pyramid/Cell of 13" that draws on what some people call "multilevel marketing" and others call a "pyramid scheme." To date, his business is small—about one hundred members—but growing. Although his Pyramid/Cell of 13 is his own creation, he, too, believes that 13 is the (suppressed) key to an enlightened perspective on the world: "Thirteen is the number of creation. Rather than avoiding it, as we have been taught, it is time to embrace 13 for the unique power and potential that it releases."

Quite a few people who wrote to me tried to convince me that understanding 13 is essential to understanding—well, just about everything. I wish I believed them. Here is one respondent's explanation of the nature of the universe and 13's place in it.

> Apparently, the whole nature of (this) Universe is being expressed as a system of 6 opposing polarities comprising the multidimensional reality-matrix. This is a very static yin/yang system if left alone; it simply cyclically re-expresses itself by recycling itself.... Number 13 introduces the New element into the Old story and therefore symbolizes the EVOLUTION (and thereby the center) of the System of 12. It most wonderfully embodies the Change. Change, as such, is not a bad thing; however, the Powers That Be are particularly famous for being resistant to Change. The great tool they apparently use to keep away the evolution and avoid the change is to mass-project the idea of them being bad for you. And there You go: number 13 is The Unlucky Number.

The nineteenth-century pioneers of triskaidekaphilia, the Thirteen Club, which embraced lucky 13 as a way of counteracting the popularity of unlucky 13, would undoubtedly have viewed their twenty-first-century heirs with bewilderment. Their goal was a rationalistic society free from superstition. If Captain William Fowler were alive today, he would probably dismiss fading conventional superstitions like unlucky 13, black cats, and open ladders as unworthy targets—and instead train his sights on the self-aggrandizing paranoia of conspiracy theorists and the incoherent mysticism of neopaganists as the real threats to a rational society.

CHAPTER ELEVEN

13 Phobes & Philes

Friday the 13th may not be exactly unlucky, but it hasn't
done us a whole lot of good.

—Will Rogers, *New York Times*, February 14, 1931

THE NEWSPAPER CLIPPINGS of an anonymous nineteenth-
century newshound led me to the realization that, despite
unlucky 13's staying power, we are in fact living in the superstition's twilight years. The creator of *Miscellany* belonged to the
golden age of triskaidekaphobia—the period between 1860 and
1940. The history of unlucky 13 in its golden age was anything but
static: fear of 13 at a table gave way to fears of Friday the 13th and
the 13th floor; people forgot where the superstition came from
and invented new explanations for the phenomenon; the word
triskaidekaphobia itself made its first appearance. It was hard not
to feel a little nostalgia for a time when people from all walks of

life debated whether or not 13 was unlucky—most of them believed it was—and newspapers were filled with accounts of the antics of the Thirteen Club. Most of the famous triskaidekaphobes mentioned in newspaper articles on unlucky 13 are from this period. For each of the triskaidekaphobes that follow there were millions of others—some equally well known, most lost to history—who also feared 13. It is no coincidence that 1860–1940 was also the golden age of triskaidekaphilia—the era when it took true independence of mind to disavow the power of 13 and embrace it as lucky. Some of their contemporaries would have called the triskaidekaphiles that follow brave; others would have called them foolhardy. This was, simply put, the time when 13 mattered most.

P. T. BARNUM (1810–1891)

P. T. Barnum, the great showman and entrepreneur, devoted an entire chapter of his 1869 autobiography, *Struggles and Triumphs*, to a discussion of unlucky 13. Only during triskaidekaphobia's golden age would "Curious Coincidence—Number Thirteen" have seemed like a reasonable choice of subject to readers of an autobiography—which explains why most modern editions of *Struggles and Triumphs* omit the chapter entirely. In chapter 44, Barnum tried to come to terms with how often 13 had turned up in his life in recent years. "Many persons are exceedingly superstitious in regard to the number 'thirteen.'. . . With regard to this number, to which so many superstitions cling, I have some interesting experiences and curious coincidences, which are worth relating as part of my personal history."

Barnum was clearly spooked by 13. He described how, despite his best efforts to hold the number at bay, he was given Room 13 again and again at hotels across the country. He described how he made two separate donations to a local church, and afterwards realized that the donations totaled $1,300.00. At around the same time, he attended a fair given by a temperance organization with two of his granddaughters and discovered after arriving back home that "in spite of my expressed determination to the contrary, I had expended exactly 'thirteen' dollars!" In the summer of 1868—the year before *Struggles and Triumphs* was published—Barnum was careful to invite fifteen guests to a clambake he was hosting, so that if one guest canceled, there would still be fourteen people at the table. "Of course, one man and his wife were 'disappointed,' and could not go—and my party numbered thirteen." That Christmas, Barnum again tried to keep 13 from the table. "I expressly arranged to have a high chair placed at the table, and my youngest grandchild, seventeen months old, was placed in it, so that we should number fourteen. After the dinner was over, we discovered that my son-in-law, Thompson, had been detained down town, and the number at the dinner table, notwithstanding my extra precautions, was exactly thirteen." The fact that Barnum didn't notice his son-in-law's absence during the entire Christmas dinner doesn't say much about what he thought of him—but he probably liked Thompson even less after he was forced to brave unlucky 13 at a table again.

At the end of "Curious Coincidences—Number Thirteen," Barnum described the events that seem to have triggered his preoccupation with 13. "Thirteen was certainly an ominous number for me in 1865, for on the thirteenth of July, the American Museum was burned to the ground, while the thirteenth of November saw the opening of 'Barnum's New Museum,' which was also subsequently destroyed by fire." In the mid- to late-nineteenth century, bad luck arriving on the 13th twice in one year would have been enough to transform even a cynical exploiter of the public's fears and obsessions like P. T. Barnum into a confirmed triskaidekaphobe. It is probably not a coincidence that every "curious coincidence" Barnum described in this chapter took place after July 13, 1865.

EDGAR ALLAN POE (1809–1849)

Edgar Allan Poe's 1839 short story "The Devil in the Belfry," a witty attack on the staid conservatism of the day, marks the author of some of the most terrifying stories ever written as a triskaidekaphile. (As does, perhaps, his marriage to his first cousin Virginia Clemm when she was thirteen years old.) The story is set in the town of Vondervotteimittiss (try saying it aloud), where residents live in accordance with the following resolutions:

> That it is wrong to alter the good old course of things.
> That there is nothing tolerable out of Vondervotteimittiss.
> That we will stick by our clocks and our cabbages.

"The pride and wonder of the village" is the clock in the belfry above the Town Council house; the residents mark the time of day by the tolling of its bell. One morning the Devil decides to shake things up in Vondervotteimittiss. He ambles into town just before noon, beats up the belfry man, and at precisely 12:00 rings the steeple bell 13 times. The Vondervotteimittissites are stunned, their world turned upside down.

"The Devil in the Belfry" was a play on the popular superstition that a clock striking 13 portended a death in the family. Gently satirizing the public's fear of 13, "The Devil in the Belfry" became one of Poe's best-known stories. Its popularity was such that almost ninety years after his death, the *New York Times* alluded to the "famous tale" when it reported that Germany had joined France and Italy in adopting the twenty-four-hour clock for railroads, postal offices, and telegraphs, thereby making the Vondervotteimittissites' nightmare—a clock striking 13 times—a reality.

"The Devil in the Belfry" was not Poe's only connection to 13. When he enrolled at the University of Virginia in 1826 (he dropped out that same year after running out of money), he was assigned Room 13. The room is now the Poe Room, a permanent exhibit that re-creates a student room circa 1826 and includes Poe's original bed from his home in Richmond. The Poe Room is the charge and favorite haunt of the Raven Society, the oldest and most prestigious honorary society at the University of Virginia. It is where new members learn that they have been elected to the society (after receiving cryptic messages that instruct them to visit on a certain day at a certain time), and it is where the initiation ceremony takes place. But, as is often the case when it comes to 13, things may not be as straightforward as they appear.

According to a local authority on the Raven Society, there is evidence that Poe moved out of Room 13 almost immediately to escape a troublesome roommate, and actually spent most of his ten months at UVA in Room 17. Unfortunately, a fire in 1895 destroyed most of the university's housing records, so it is unlikely that the mystery of Room 13 will ever be solved.

BAYARD TAYLOR (1825–1878)

The American idea that 13 cannot be unlucky because of its significance in U.S. history is an old one. In the nineteenth century, after the rise of unlucky 13, skeptics made the same argument. Then as now, the implication was that believing in unlucky 13 was tantamount to being unpatriotic. But in the nineteenth century the superstition was too strong to be affected. Besides, for true believers, there was always another way to look at things. During the Civil War, one famous triskaidekaphobe with Union sympathies provided a topical rebuttal to this patriotic appeal. Bayard Taylor, like many accomplished people of that era, was a generalist. An intrepid traveler and travel writer at a time when both were unusual—his first travelogue, published in 1846, was entitled *Views Afoot: or, Europe Seen With Knapsack and Staff*—Taylor was also a respected poet and diplomat. In 1863, when he was the U.S. chargé d'affaires in Russia, he hosted a dinner in St. Petersburg commemorating George Washington's birthday. In his speech, he made the patriot's case for unlucky 13. His counterargument to the sanctity of the 13 colonies was simple: just as there had been a Judas among the 13 who sat down at the Last Supper, there was a

Judas among the 13 original colonies: South Carolina, the first state to secede from the Union. After South Carolina "betrayed" the United States following Lincoln's election in November 1860, Mississippi, Florida, Alabama, Georgia, Louisiana, and Texas quickly followed suit—and the Confederate States of America was born. In Bayard Taylor's view, the original 13 colonies not only did not refute unlucky 13, they were further evidence that the number carried a curse.

MATTHEW ARNOLD (1822–1888)

At least one prominent triskaidekaphile who was determined to undo unlucky 13 inadvertently advanced the enemy's cause. The Victorian poet and cultural critic Matthew Arnold braved 13 at a table in 1887 to prove the superstition wrong, despite the fact that his health was so poor that he had recently been obliged to give up his position at Oxford University. When he died within a year, triskaidekaphobes the world over took it as confirmation that when it came to 13, it was unwise to tempt fate. Nor was Arnold's fate quickly forgotten. A 1910 book called *The Origins of Superstitions and Customs* observed: "When the daring of Matthew Arnold in defying the superstition is told in all its solemnity... even solid people shudder and begin to think 'there is something in it.'" The influence of Matthew Arnold on the 13-at-a-table superstition was still felt in the United Kingdom in 1930, as evidenced by a cigarette card printed by Godfrey Phillips cigarettes that year as part of their "Popular Superstitions" series. The following sentence made it onto the back of the tiny card: "The number of adherents to this superstition was greatly augmented when Matthew Arnold defied it and died within a year."

GENERAL JOHN ALEXANDER LOGAN (1826–1886)

John Alexander Logan, a celebrated Civil War general, is chiefly remembered today as the person responsible for Memorial Day becoming a national holiday. In 1886, General Logan was the senior senator from the state of Illinois. That year, while attending an important social function, he discovered that he was to be one of 13 people at dinner. The celebrated veteran promptly told his host that he preferred to sit at a side table rather than tempt unlucky 13, and his host obliged. But the precaution was to no avail; Logan died within the year.

OSCAR WILDE (1854–1900)

Like many notable figures of his day, Oscar Wilde received an invitation to attend a Thirteen Club dinner as a guest of honor. In his polite but firm reply to Lewis Waller, founder of the London Thirteen Club, Wilde explained that although he believed 13 to be a lucky number, he could not accept. Wilde rejected the didacticism of the Thirteen Club's mission and, ever the iconoclast, saw more beauty than danger in superstition: "I love superstitions. They are the colour element of thought and imagination. They are the opponents of common sense. Common sense is the enemy of romance."

13 MORE PHOBES & PHILES

Phobes:

1

Gioacchino Rossini, Italian composer (1792–1868)

2

Edward VII, king of England (1841–1910)

3

Sergei Diaghilev, Russian ballet impresario (1872–1929)

4

H. L. Mencken, editor and journalist (1880–1956)

5

Franklin Delano Roosevelt, president of the United States
(1882–1945)

6

J. Paul Getty, business executive (1892–1976)

7

Marion Davies, actress (1897–1961)

8

Tennessee Williams, playwright (1911–1983)

9

Truman Capote, author (1924–1984)

Philes:

10

Florenz Ziegfeld, theatrical producer (1869–1932)

11

Lilly Dache, milliner (1898–1989)

12

Bill Monroe, musician (1911–1996)

13

Lawrence Durrell, author (1912–1990)

ELLA WHEELER WILCOX (1850–1919)

Ella Wheeler Wilcox, the fabulously successful sentimental poet who penned the famous lines "Laugh, and the world laughs with you; Weep, and you weep alone" shared her massive readership's distrust of 13. At a Thirteen Club dinner in 1902, honoring the Vegetarian Society of New York, the chief ruler read aloud from a letter she had sent, declining their invitation to attend: "I don't like thirteen . . . I believe in the power of concentrated thought: it has favored for hundreds of years thirteen as unlucky. I am glad you are making a counter-current. In a hundred years or so it will overcome the other wave. Then I will dine with you." Given her well-publicized, enthusiastic interest in spiritualism—in later years, she communicated with her deceased husband using a Ouija board—it is possible that she meant to keep the date. Her belief in unlucky 13 was especially fervent because the only time she attended a dinner of 13, the host died a few months later.

GEORGE EASTMAN (1854–1932)

If George Eastman, the founder of Eastman Kodak, had had his way, there would now be 13 months in a year, 28 days in a month, and a Friday the 13th in every one. Two decades before Sophia Vembo's 13 Month World Calendar was unveiled at the First American Exhibition on Superstition, Prejudice and Fear in 1948, Eastman spearheaded an international movement for calendar reform, which he described as his "one hobby." Eastman contended that the current calendar wreaked havoc with business practices, especially accounting and payroll, and that a new calendar system was essential to the advancement of the economy. The calendar he favored—the Cotsworth Calendar—had first been proposed by Moses B. Cotsworth in 1888, thirty-nine years after the great French mathematician Auguste Comte proposed his own 13-month calendar based on his "Church of Humanity" (each month to be named after one of history's great men: Moses, Shakespeare, Descartes, etc.). Eastman's influence and financial muscle gave the idea new life. He was particularly concerned about the variations in the length of each month—they caused problems for month-to-month productivity analyses—and the variation in the number of weeks per month. He also objected to the phenomenon of "wandering" holidays—holidays that appear on different days in different years—and singled out Easter as being particularly worrisome.

Eastman and Cotsworth's proposed calendar had the advantage of having each month be of equal length, with the same date falling on the same day of the week each month—including the 13th. Well aware of the prevalence of the Friday the 13th superstition (and the vociferous resistance a calendar with 13 Friday the 13ths would face), Eastman attempted to tap into the long-dead patriotic association of 13 with the original 13 colonies. Despite his best efforts to convince the public that 13 months with 13 Friday the 13ths would be a wonderful way to honor the nation's history, it was an impossible sell. It did not help Eastman's cause any that his proposal created new complications, and not just for triskaidekaphobes. In addition to the 13th month, Sol, which would be inserted between June and July, the calendar required the addition of something called "Year Day" between Saturday, December 28, and Sunday, January 1, which would carry neither a number nor a day of the week, and a second new blank day in the leap year between Saturday, June 28, and the first day of Sol. When George Eastman committed suicide in 1932, the 13-month calendar lost its most vocal supporter and its biggest source of funding. Calendar reform continued to be a significant international movement until the late 1930s, when deteriorating political conditions in Europe effectively killed it.

ARNOLD SCHOENBERG (1874–1951)

Austrian classical composer Arnold Schoenberg was born on September 13, 1874, and died on July 13, 1951. In between, he was a dedicated triskaidekaphobe. According to the former archivist of the now-defunct Arnold Schoenberg Institute at the University of Southern California—the institute's collection was moved to Vienna in 1998—Schoenberg often omitted page number 13 from his musical scores, replacing it with 12b. His unfinished opera, *Moses and Aron*, was originally entitled *Moses and Aaron*, until someone pointed out that the title contained 13 letters. As a septuagenarian, Schoenberg worried that he would not live past 76 (7 + 6 = 13). He was right—but in 1951, 76 was a pretty good run.

WOODROW WILSON (1856–1924)

President Woodrow Wilson was one of the most famous figures to embrace 13, and he did so on a very public stage. In 1912, when he was governor of New Jersey, a presidential hopeful, and an honorary member of the Thirteen Club, Wilson told reporters: "Thirteen is a lucky number for me. I'm not afraid of 13. You know there are thirteen letters in my name, and in my thirteenth year at Princeton University I became its thirteenth President. Thirteen has been my lucky number right along." After this admission, whenever an occasion involved both Wilson and the number 13, reference was invariably made to it being his lucky number. When he remarried in 1915, while president, the *New York Times* noted that his was the fourteenth license issued that day, and that he had missed his lucky number by only a few minutes. Posthumously, Wilson's luck almost held. In 1925, his face almost made it onto the 13-cent stamp. The options were a 17-cent stamp or a 13-cent stamp; given recent increases in postal rates, the former was needed for parcel-post mailings and the latter for registered mail. The decision came down to the wire, but in the end, Wilson ended up with 17, dressed in memorial black. (The 13-cent stamp went to former President Harrison.)

HERBERT HOOVER (1874–1964)

Unlike Chester Arthur, Benjamin Harrison, Grover Cleveland, Theodore Roosevelt, and Woodrow Wilson before him, Herbert Hoover's name never made the roll call of honorary members of the Thirteen Club. The 31st president of the United States was known to be a triskaidekaphobe. Perhaps Hoover had reason to be wary of 13. Thirteen books were written about him in 1932, the year he ran for reelection and lost—most of them critical assessments of his first term. In his successful presidential campaign four years earlier, a Democratic senator tried to exploit his fear of 13 by asking him to answer 13 questions about what he would do, if elected. This bold tactic rated national headlines; however, it did not keep Hoover from winning the presidency.

LILY PONS (1898–1976)

Lily Pons, the celebrated coloratura soprano of the 1930s through 1950s who had a town in Maryland and a locomotive named after her, was a birthday triskaidekaphile. Born on Friday the 13th, she decided at an early age that 13 was her lucky number. Throughout her career she sought out hotel rooms on the 13th floor and Pullman car number 13. Her home address was 13 Silvermine Road. She even refused to accept the marriage proposal of Andre Kostelanetz, her second husband, until he asked 13 times.

ADOLF HITLER (1889–1945)

In 1934, Chancellor Adolf Hitler made official Germany's rejection of the proposed 13-month calendar, promoted by the late George Eastman, for the same reasons expressed by other countries: the cost and confusion inherent in such a drastic change. But he was reported to have had another, more personal reason: fear of 13. That year, a Canadian journalist noted in the *Journal of Calendar Reform*: "It cannot be said that the Chancellor is superstitious, but he has a 'healthy respect' for numbers. And one that he does not like is 'thirteen.'"

CHAPTER TWELVE

Triskaidekaphobe's Travel Guide

> Avoid being thirteen at table; it brings bad luck. The skeptics should not fail to joke: "What's the difference? I'll eat enough for two!" Or again, if there are ladies present, ask if any is pregnant.
>
> —Gustave Flaubert, *Dictionary of Received Ideas* (1911)

S INCE THE MIDDLE of the nineteenth century, books and articles have consistently labeled unlucky 13 the most popular superstition in the world. However, there has never been a list of triskaidekaphobic countries to confirm this. To correct this oversight, I decided to contact representatives at all the foreign embassies in Washington, D.C., and ask each of them if their country had a history of the superstition. Unlucky 13, it turns out, is nearly as ubiquitous as Christianity itself. A triskaidekaphobe who wants a vacation from the contemporary insurgence of triskaidekaphilia has many options. The following countries confirmed the presence of the unlucky 13 tradition in their cultures:

Argentina	Cuba	Iceland	Romania
Australia	Czech Republic	Ireland	Russia
Austria	Denmark	Lebanon	South Africa
Belarus	Ecuador	Lithuania	Spain
Belgium	El Salvador	Mexico	Sweden
Belize	Estonia	The Netherlands	Switzerland
Bolivia	Fiji	New Zealand	United Kingdom
Brazil	Finland	Norway	
Bulgaria	France	Pakistan	
Canada	Georgia	Peru	
Chile	Germany	Philippines	
Costa Rica	Guatemala	Poland	
Croatia	Hungary	Portugal	

A handful of embassies reported that their countries were not afflicted with fear of 13: China, India, Indonesia, Italy, Japan, Korea, and Saudi Arabia. Three of these countries reported other number superstitions, and two of them—Italy and China—reported established traditions of triskaidekaphilia.

While unlucky 13 is a constant throughout much of the world, there is considerable variation from country to country in the relative presence, absence, and popularity of specific 13 superstitions. Air Canada, British Airways, and Virgin Airways include Row 13 in their aircraft; Air France and Lufthansa do not. The missing-13th-floor phenomenon is common in Canada,

New Zealand, the United Kingdom, and Brazil, but uncommon in Switzerland, Bulgaria, and the Netherlands. In many countries, 13 at a table has faded considerably, but in Switzerland, it still has a significant presence. People in the Philippines also avoid 13 at a table, but the *Trece Martires* (Thirteen Martyrs)—13 Filipino revolutionaries who were executed by the Spaniards during the Philippine Revolution of 1896—are not considered an historical example of unlucky 13, nor is the city of the same name. In Estonia, Lithuania, and Scotland, 13 is known as the "devil's dozen"—an expression derived from John (6:70): "Have not I chosen you twelve, and one of you is a devil?" In the nineteenth century, "devil's dozen" was also popular in the United States, but today it is all but forgotten. Australia and the United States share many of the same 13 superstitions; however, in Australia the 13th day of the month is still considered unlucky even when it doesn't fall on Friday, and Australian cricket players call eighty-seven the "devil's number" because it is 13 short of one hundred. Throughout much of Europe, it is considered bad luck to present someone with 13 flowers; while it would be considered odd (and unlucky by some) to do so in the United States, it is not a conventional 13 superstition.

Superstitions are malleable; they change with exposure to the beliefs and experiences of different cultures. In the case of number superstitions, which by their nature invite application to a wide variety of phenomena, no two countries will share the same set of superstitions with the same degree of prevalence at any given time. One of the most significant international variations in unlucky 13 is which 13th day of the month is unluckiest.

Most countries bestow that honor upon Friday, but a significant minority favors Tuesday. The Thirteen Club noted this difference in 1893; at the eleventh annual dinner of the club, one of the speakers shared with the audience his discovery that Tuesday, not Friday, was the unlucky day in Spain. In most Latin countries, Tuesday the 13th is considered the unluckiest day of the year. This belief is captured by the popular expression, *En trece y martes, ni te cases ni te embarques* (On Tuesday the 13th, don't marry or embark on a trip). Tuesday the 13th is also considered unlucky in Greece and Romania.

The phenomenon of unlucky Tuesday the 13th in Spain makes for an interesting case study in the migration of superstitions—and the cultural imperialism of American cinema. In the wake of the *Friday the 13th* movies, Friday the 13th has emerged in Spain as a competitor to the indigenous Tuesday the 13th superstition. Many Spaniards now believe that Friday the 13th is the unlucky 13, even though the superstition has no roots in their culture. Others consider both Tuesday the 13th and Friday the 13th unlucky. Anecdotal evidence suggests that Friday the 13th is becoming more popular in Spain and may even constitute a threat to the future of unlucky Tuesday the 13th. Some Spaniards object to the adoption of a foreign superstition as a betrayal of their own cultural heritage. Of course, the confusion could have been avoided entirely if the film's distributors had named the Spanish version *Martes 13* and changed the two brief Friday references in the movie to Tuesday—but they stuck with *Viernes 13*, which made about as much sense to the Spanish as *Monday the 27th* would to us. It is amazing how much impact a single individual's decision can have on another country's cultural beliefs—all the more amazing when that impact is entirely unintentional. A decision twenty-five years ago by an American film producer to change the title of a slasher movie from *Long Night at Camp Blood* to *Friday the 13th* is responsible for an ongoing battle between competing superstitions in a country thousands of miles away—a battle that will ultimately decide which date on the calendar millions of people consider the most inauspicious.

THE "OTHER" THIRTEEN CLUBS

Writing in the 1860s, the well-traveled P. T. Barnum observed that fear of 13 was most evident in Catholic countries. He attributed this to the Last Supper. Although 13 was considered an unlucky number throughout Europe, he singled out France as especially stricken. In the 1820s, unlucky 13 at a table was already pervasive enough in France to be the subject of a song by the celebrated French poet, Pierre Jean de Béranger. In *"Treize à Table,"* a man discovers that he is one of 13 at a dinner table. He looks down and sees that he has spilled the salt. (This was an allusion to Leonardo da Vinci's painting the *Last Supper*, which depicts Judas having knocked over the salt.) He cries out, *"Nombre fatal! Présage épouvantable!"* ("Fatal number! Terrible omen!") At that moment, he is visited by a vision of Death. Instead of a skeleton or hooded figure with a sickle, Death is a woman—beautiful, young, and smiling. The man realizes that no one who believes in God need fear Death. Unlike most later writing that addresses the 13 superstition in a fictional context, *"Treize à Table"* accepts the superstition that 13 at a table is unlucky—mortally so—on its own terms. The song does not dispute the effect of sitting 13 at a table; instead, it suggests that only a godless man need fear it. Béranger's song was popular in the United Kingdom and United States, as well as France, and in *Extraordinary Popular Delusions*, published the following decade, Charles Mackay deemed it "exquisite" and praised its "lesson of genuine wisdom."

Given France's early commitment to reducing fear of 13 at a table, perhaps it is not surprising that the earliest Thirteen Club on record is found not in New York, but in France. Embedded in a summary of news from Paris in an 1858 *New York Times* article is a description of a recently formed "Society of Thirteen" in Bordeaux, which met every Friday, 13 at a table, to challenge the superstition. "Before sitting down these courageous men will turn their chairs around, then turn over their salt-cellars, place in the form of a cross their knives and forks, and at dessert break a looking glass." The *Times* implies that the 13 superstition was even more popular in France than in the United States, and concludes admiringly, "The project of the thirteen Bordelais is an act of heroism, nothing more or less." Although nineteenth-century U.S. sources credit Captain Fowler with inventing the Thirteen Club, given the parallels between the French and U.S. clubs, it is all but certain that he used the earlier Bordeaux club as his model.

The French Thirteen Club had no better luck dethroning 13 at a table than the New York club did. Two decades after the notice in the *Times*, Edmond Audran's opera, *La Mascotte*, which premiered in Paris in 1880, included the following lines: "*Jamais on ne devrait | Se mettre à table treize, | Mais douze c'est parfait*"

("Never put 13 at a table, But twelve, that is perfect.") Seventy years later, when the superstition was on its last legs in the United States, it was still alive and well in France. In 1953, it was the subject of a hit play, *Treize à Table*, by Marc-Gilbert Sauvajon, which was made into a movie in 1956 and has been revived many times since.

Although the 13-at-a-table superstition may have originated in England, its nemesis, the Thirteen Club, definitely did not. London's Thirteen Club was modeled on the New York Thirteen Club. Dinners featured 13 guests to a table, broken mirrors, crossed silverware, open ladders, macabre party favors, and illustrious members. The founder and president of the London Thirteen Club was the well-known journalist William Harnett Blanch, and the chairman was the brilliant *Punch* illustrator Harry Furniss. The London club was no more successful than the New York or Bordeaux clubs in wiping out unlucky 13 at a table. In 1930, the English cigarette manufacturer Godfrey Phillips issued a series of 25 cigarette cards called "Popular Superstitions." Card 18 was a depiction of "Thirteen At Table." The card shows a party of 13 with a servant rounding the corner with a tray; one of the 13, a young women in a fashionable green dress, has just stood up, frightened by the discovery that she is one of the fateful number. A description on the back of the card includes a brief note on the prevalence of the superstition: "Perhaps of all superstitions none has greater strength to-day than that which holds that if thirteen people sit down to table one of them will die within a year."

Unlucky 13 does not appear to have followed a clear path of progress around the world, spreading slowly from country to country and region to region. In most triskaidekaphobic countries, 13 exploded onto the scene, as it did in the United States, in the early and mid-nineteenth century. The earliest references were to the 13-at-a-table superstition. By mid-century, references to other 13 superstitions were finding their way into foreign newspapers and literature. A *New York Times* article from 1880 confirms that unlucky 13 was a well-known international phenomenon by then: "[It] is not confined to any particular nation or civilization, though it is not a pagan, but a Christian superstition.... In Roman Catholic countries the superstition ... is generally prevalent, and so firmly held that it would be well-nigh impossible to induce 13 persons to sit down at dinner." Most other triskaidekaphobic cultures today still attribute their belief in unlucky 13 to the influence of the Last Supper, and in general, they are less familiar with the alternative theories that emerged in the twentieth century than people in the United States.

OTHER CULTURES, OTHER NUMBERS

Most cultures have a tradition of number superstitions, even cultures in which triskaidekaphobia does not have a presence. In Indonesia, for example, where 13 is not unlucky, the unluckiest number is 12; where we say *unlucky 13*, they say *celaka 12*. Probably the most popular number superstition in the world after 13 is fear of the number four—*tesserophobia*. The number four is considered extremely unlucky in China, Taiwan, Japan, and Korea, and is a much more popular superstition in those countries than unlucky 13 is in the West. Their number superstitions operate according to a different principle than unlucky 13. Where in the West 13 is a cultural superstition that emerged as a reinterpretation of a religious belief, in Asia unlucky four is a function of linguistics. In Chinese, Japanese, and Korean, the word for *four* is, unfortunately, an exact homonym for *death*.

Not surprisingly, China, Taiwan, Japan, and Korea have long-established traditions of four omission in their architecture and design. According to a representative at Otis Elevators, the world's largest manufacturer, installer, and servicer of elevators, the practice of omitting the fourth floor is more common in Asia than the practice of omitting the 13th floor in the West. Another indication of the prevalence of unlucky four in Asia can be found in Northwest Airlines's policies for aisle omission. While Northwest does not omit the 13th row on any of its domestic or international aircraft, its Asian fleet omits the fourth row. Northwest clearly believes that it is more likely to encounter tesserophobes in Asia than triskaidekaphobes elsewhere.

Making matters worse, in Chinese the word for *one* sounds the same as the word for *must*; the word for *fourteen*, therefore, sounds like the phrase *must die*. This is why the fourteenth floor is also often omitted in Asian architecture. Twenty-four is also avoided because the word for *two* sounds the same as the word for *easy*, making *twenty-four* a homonym for *easy to die*. In light of the connection between four and death, it is only natural that number superstitions are taken more seriously in Asia than in the West; no shift in cultural beliefs will change the fact that every time millions of people say the word for *four*, they are also saying the word for *death*. A recent article in the *China Daily* shows the extent to which the Chinese will go to avoid four. In April 2004, in the Guandong Province in South China, the government agency that issues license plates decided to stop offering plates with the number four on them in an attempt cut down on traffic accidents. Even during the golden age of triskaidekaphobia in the United States, license plates were issued with the number 13. (This is not to say that the public was happy about it. In 1903, the chief of police in Fort Wayne, Indiana, reported that "vehicle license tag No. 13" was often refused or returned.)

Tesserophobia is even strong enough to affect architecture and design in cultures where it is not an indigenous belief— including in triskaidekaphobic cultures. In Vancouver, Canada, which has a large Asian population, it is easier to find a 13th floor than a floor with the number four in it. According to a local architect, "None of the houses or apartments built by or for the Asian population will have a four anywhere, so no fourth, fourteenth, or twenty-fourth floors, no rooms with the number four, and no street addresses with four."

There is an upside to the potency of Asian number superstitions. For the same reason that four is considered unlucky, certain numbers are considered extremely lucky—luckier than any number in Western culture. In China, the number eight is as lucky as four is unlucky; this is because the Chinese word for *eight* is a homonym for the word for *lucky*. The same phonetic coincidence is responsible for making 13 a lucky number: the Chinese word for 13 sounds the same as the phrase *must succeed*. In Hong Kong, cellphone users request 13 because of the good luck it brings.

In the West, Italy succeeded where so many countries in the nineteenth and twentieth centuries failed: even during the golden age of triskaidekaphobia, it managed to keep unlucky 13 at bay. A century after Christianity's benevolent 13 fell to unlucky 13 at a table, Italians still associated 13 with the benevolence of Christ and his twelve disciples, and with December 13th, St. Lucia's day. Italian-American immigrants have been a consistent triskaidekaphilic influence in the United States for generations. Long before lucky 13 charms and pendants became popular, Italian-Americans wore them proudly. But this does not mean that Italy is any more immune to number superstitions than the United States. In Italy, 17 is considered an unlucky number, and Friday the 17th an unlucky day.

CHAPTER THIRTEEN

The Future of 13

SUPERSTITION. That which survives when its companions are dead.

—E. Cobham Brewer, *Dictionary of Phrase and Fable* (1870)

T HE RELATIVELY BRIEF history of unlucky 13, and its rise and fall as the world's most popular superstition, is a useful reminder that neither reason nor historical precedent is necessary for a belief to win over the world, or to fall from grace. Over the course of three centuries, 13 has come full circle: from the positive 13 of the Church and the founding fathers to the negative 13 of the nineteenth and twentieth centuries, and back to the positive 13 of neopagans, contrarians, and conspiracy theorists. One of the lessons of unlucky 13 is that it is impossible to predict the future of a cultural belief or superstition. A Christian in the Middle Ages would have been horrified to discover that the benevolent 13 of

Christ and his twelve disciples would one day be transformed into the unluckiest number in the world. George Washington and his contemporaries would have been shocked to learn that their 13, proud symbol of the new United States of America, would within fifty years emerge as the country's most feared superstition. Both the late-nineteenth-century triskaidekaphobe and the social critic who mocked him would have been surprised to learn that in the twentieth century, 13 at a table had unceremoniously faded away, only to be replaced by a new 13 superstition: Friday the 13th. Thirteen Clubbers would no doubt have appreciated the irony that in the twenty-first century a *lucky* 13 superstition has become the most significant threat to their nemesis—but they would have been disappointed that superstition itself has endured.

Unlucky 13 survives today less as a national superstition than as national awareness of a superstition. The awareness that people think 13 is unlucky is nearly universal, even as the number of people who actually believe the superstition continues to decline. The original 13 superstition—13 at a table—is already extinct. Friday the 13th is fading, too—but not as quickly as the other unlucky 13s. Perennial TV and newspaper stories continue to keep it in the public eye. If the trend continues, it is likely that fear of Friday the 13th will become the only remaining vestige of what was once a diverse array of 13 superstitions. Thirteen will again have come full circle—from one superstition to many, and back to one again.

It is impossible to predict the future of 13—but it is still fun to try. Eventually, radio stations and newspapers will stop commenting on the arrival of unlucky Friday the 13th; and before long, it, too, will become extinct. By the end of this century, all that will be left of unlucky 13 will be an urban landscape of high-rises without 13th floors. The missing 13th floor—an architectural anachronism that makes people shake their heads and think, Are people *still* so superstitious?—will be its lasting legacy. A fear that once terrorized and transformed the world will be reduced to momentary incredulity. There will, of course, always be a smattering of triskaidekaphobes. The mere fact that unlucky 13 was for a time the most popular superstition in the world will keep it alive as a significant number in the minds of many—and as an unlucky number in the minds of some. As long as there are people who believe in good and bad luck, 13 will always have a place in the pantheon of unlucky numbers. But it will amount to little more than another individual number superstition.

In the future, triskaidekaphilia will continue to fare better than triskaidekaphobia. Fueled by the Internet, the ever-increasing popularity of neopagan and New Age beliefs is converting more people to triskaidekaphilia every day. One reason for lucky 13's resilience is its ability to withstand the onslaught of contemporary anti-superstitionists. Even today there are people who, like the Thirteen Clubbers and the postwar alarmists, are truly incensed by the fact that some people still consider 13 to be unlucky. They are convinced that superstition eats away at the fabric of reason and they argue that it must be stamped out whenever and wherever it appears. Instead of seeing in unlucky 13 what Oscar Wilde called "the colour element of thought and imagination," they see a potential conflagration that could at any moment send our society back to the Dark Ages. Lucky 13 is less likely to be targeted by this contingent than unlucky 13 because as a culture we have always been much less inclined to view positive superstitions as insidious.

One day not too long ago, I set aside the number 13 for a little while and picked up *Miscellany*, the scrapbook to which I owe my accidental interest in numerology. I opened it at random and saw another article I had never seen before. Published on June 7, 1878, in the *New York Times*, "The Westchester Murder" described the discovery of the body of one George Howard, a bank robber and former hotel proprietor who had been shot twice in the head a few days earlier and dumped at the Westchester-Bronx border by person or persons unknown. I turned the page and found a long detailed account of a bank robbery, complete with diagrams: "A Great Bank Robbery. The Manhattan Savings Institution Robbed. Three Millions and a Half in Cash and Securities Stolen...." I noted that the bank robbery had taken place in October 1878, more than four months after George Howard's murder, and assumed it was a coincidence that both articles were on the same subject. But when I turned the page I changed my mind. For only the second time, I had discovered a series of related articles in *Miscellany*. The third article was dated October 6, 1879. By then, "A Great Bank Robbery" had become "The Great Bank Robbery"—the stuff of legend. The article mentioned that George Howard, alias George Leonidas Leslie, had been, until his untimely murder at the age of forty-four, a member of the gang that had planned and carried out the Manhattan Savings

Institution heist, "one of the most daring and successful burglaries ever perpetrated."

I felt momentarily betrayed by my anonymous benefactor. I knew it was unlikely that the creator of *Miscellany* was both a member of the Thirteen Club *and* a member of the gang that had robbed the Manhattan Savings Institution. And I now realized that I had no more reason to suspect that he was a member of one than the other. Much as I wanted to believe that he was a part of the Thirteen Club—probably a key member, a *chief ruler*—I realized it was much more likely that he simply found certain subjects more interesting than others, and had applied his scissors and glue accordingly.

The little information there was in *Miscellany* on George Leonidas Leslie aroused my curiosity. Leslie's life and career were truly extraordinary. An erudite, charismatic figure who enjoyed high society as much as robbing banks, Leslie was a brilliant strategist and an expert safecracker. He was no ordinary bank robber; he was the leader and mastermind of the most successful gang of bank robbers in U.S. history. Although he did not live to reap the rewards, he planned the Manhattan Savings Institution robbery and dozens of other successful heists. Commenting on the exploits of the "Leslie gang," George W. Walling, New York City's chief of police at the time, estimated, "Throughout the United States their plunderings cannot have been less than $7,000,000, comprising 80 per cent. of all the bank robberies perpetrated from 1860 to the date of Leslie's death." Leslie's reputation in the underworld was such that he was hired as a consultant by other gangs around the country, advising them on prospective jobs in return for a share of the loot.

Adding to his legend is the fact that his murder was never solved. Although no one has published a biography of George Leonidas Leslie, several twentieth-century books have touched on his life, including two celebrated books on New York crime, Herbert Asbury's *Gangs of New York* and Luc Sante's *Low Life*. Both books accomplish the miraculous feat of extending Leslie's life of crime by six full years. Despite numerous articles in New York papers attesting to Leslie's demise in 1878, both books state that he was found murdered in June 1884 and, even more impressively, manage to describe some of his criminal exploits in the years in between. In fairness to Asbury and Sante, their source was no less a personage than George W. Walling, who got the date wrong in his memoir. Only a long-forgotten and out-of-print book, *Murders Not Quite Solved*, managed to avoid the red herring and keep its facts straight.

In the end, what surprised me most about the story of unlucky 13 was not how pervasive the superstition was or how it evolved or even where it came from, but how much our shared beliefs about its history diverge from the historical record. How could so many newspaper articles and books about superstition leave out the Thirteen Club? How could so many people be off by seven centuries in their attribution of the origin of Friday the 13th, or defy decades of reputable historical research and claim that unlucky 13 was Christianity's attempt to undermine paganism's benevolent

13? Perhaps this is the lesson of unlucky 13: superstition is not an isolated country of irrational beliefs any more than the superstitious are its dim-witted, frightened citizens; reason governs a much smaller domain in the world of ideas than we are accustomed to acknowledging. In the end, to believe otherwise is simply to embrace another positive, hopeful superstition—another lucky 13.

Selected Bibliography

THERE ARE TWO main categories of source material on unlucky 13: newspaper articles and any of the dozens of dictionaries and encyclopedias of superstition that were published in the latter half of the twentieth century. Since most of these sources reproduced the same handful of "facts" about unlucky 13, and many of these "facts" were false or, at best, unverifiable, I could not depend on them to provide the foundation for the story of 13. The recent innovation of online text databases enabled me to start from scratch, and to search for references to unlucky 13 across tens of thousands of books, newspapers, and periodicals spanning eight centuries. Part of what made the research process so enjoyable was that my progress was defined as much by what I did not find as what I did; each day brought a new miscellany as varied and interesting as the one that inspired this book.

American Psychiatric Association, *Diagnostic and Statistical Manual of Mental Disorders*. Washington, D.C.: American Psychiatric Association, 1952.

American Psychiatric Association, *Diagnostic and Statistical Manual of Mental Disorders, Fourth Edition* (DSM-IV), Washington, D.C.: American Psychiatric Press, 1994.

Arbuthnot, John. *Of the Laws of Chance*. London: Printed by Benj. Motte, and sold by Randall Taylor, 1692.

Aubrey, John. *John Aubrey's Miscellanies*, 4th edition. London: John Russell Smith, 1857.

Barnum, P. T. *Struggles and Triumphs*. Hartford: J. B. Burr & Company, 1869.

Battle, Kemp. P. *Great American Folklore*. New York: Simon & Schuster, 1989.

Berlitz, Charles. *Native Tongues*. New York: Grosset & Dunlap, 1982.

Brand, John. *Observations on Popular Antiquities, including the whole of Mr. Bourne's* Antiquitates Vulgares. Newcastle upon Tyne: J. Johnson, 1777.

Brenner, Charles. *An Elementary Textbook of Psychoanalysis*. Revised edition. New York: Anchor Books, 1974.

Brewer, E. Cobham. *Dictionary of Phrase and Fable*. London: Cassell and Company, Limited, 1902.

Brodeur, Arthur Gilchrist, trans. *The Prose Edda of Snorri Sturlson*. New York: The American-Scandinavian Foundation, 1916.

Bulfinch, Thomas. *Bulfinch's Mythology*. Reprint. New York: Crown Publishers, 1978.

Burnet, Gilbert. *Some passages of the life and death of the right honourable John, Earl of Rochester who died the 26th of July, 1680*. London: Printed for Richard Chiswell, 1692.

Casas, Bartolomé de las. *A Short Account of the Destruction of the Indies*. New York: Penguin USA, 1999.

Connington, J. J. *No Past Is Dead*. Boston: Little, Brown and Company, 1942.

Coriat, Isador H. *Abnormal Psychology*. New York: Moffat, Yard and Company, 1910.

Cowell, F. R. *Everyday Life in Ancient Rome*. New York: G. P. Putnam's Sons, 1961.

Dresslar, Fletcher Bascom. "Superstition and Education," *Education*, Volume 5, No. 1, 1907.

Dudycha, George J. "The Superstitious Beliefs of College Students," *Journal of Abnormal Psychology*, 1933.

Dummett, Michael. *The Game of Tarot.* London: Gerald Duckworth & Co Ltd., 1980.

Eastman, George. "The Importance of Calendar Reform to the Business World," *Nation's Business*, May, 1926.

Echlin, Erland. "Germany's New Viewpoint," *Journal of Calendar Reform*, Vol. 3, No. 2, 1934.

Einarsson, Stefan. *A History of Icelandic Literature.* Baltimore: Johns Hopkins Press, 1957.

Encyclopedia Britannica. Twenty-four volumes. London: Encyclopedia Britannica, 1929.

Evelyn-White, Hugh G., trans. *Hesiod: Work and Days.* Massachussetts: Harvard University Press, 1914.

Flaubert, Gustave. *Bouvard and Pecuchet, with the Dictionary of Received Ideas.* London: Penguin Classics, 1976.

Frazier, James George. *The Golden Bough.* Reprint. New York: Crown Publishers, 1981.

Freud, Sigmund. *The Interpretation of Dreams.* New York: Avon, 1980.

Gardyn, Rebecca and Fetto, John. "Tempting Fate," *American Demographics*, Vol. 22, Issue 10, 2000.

Goodman, Linda. *Star Signs.* New York: St. Martin's Press, 1993.

Halleran, E. E. *Thirteen Toy Pistols.* Philadelphia: David McKay Company, 1945.

Hamilton, Edith. *Mythology.* New York: Little, Brown & Company, 1942.

Hand, Wayland D., Anna Casetta, and Sondra B. Thiederman, eds. *Popular Beliefs and Superstitions: A Compendium of American Folklore: from the Ohio Collection of Newbell Niles Puckett.* Boston: G. K. Hall and Company, 1981. (This was a key source for the 13-at-a-table superstitions on page 4 and the Friday-the-13th superstitions on page 84.)

Herbermann, Charles G., ed. *The Catholic Encyclopedia.* Fifteen volumes. New York: Robert Appleton Co., 1915.

Higgins, M. and Matoney J., et al. "The Calendar Struggle with George Eastman and Moses B. Cotsworth Versus Miss Elisabeth Achelis: A Story Worth Remembering in Accounting." Unpublished paper. 2002.

Hoffman, Paul. "Nervous on Friday the 13th?" *Smithsonian Magazine*, February, 1987.

Holland, Merlin and Hart-Davis, Rupert, eds. *The Complete Letters of Oscar Wilde.* New York: Henry Holt and Company, 2000.

Howarth, Stephen. *The Knights Templar.* New York: Atheneum, 1982.

Ifrah, Georges. *The Universal History of Numbers.* New York: John Wiley & Sons, 2000.

Jahoda, Gustav. *The Psychology of Superstition.* London: Penguin Books, 1970.

Knowlson, T. Sharper. *The Origins of Popular Superstitions and Customs.* London: T. Werner Laurie, Limited, 1910.

Lawrence, Robert Means. *The Magic of the Horse-Shoe.* Boston: Houghton, Mifflin and Company, 1898.

Lawson, Thomas W. *Friday, the Thirteenth.* New York: Doubleday, Page & Company, 1907.

Lewis, Jerry M. and Gallagher, Timothy J. "The Salience of Friday the 13th for College Students," *College Student Journal,* Vol. 35 (2), 2001.

Lindow, John. *Norse Mythology.* New York: Oxford University Press, 2001.

King, Martin Luther. *Strength to Love.* New York: HarperCollins Publishers, 1977.

MacDougall, Curtis D. *Understanding Public Opinion: A Guide for Newspapermen and Newspaper Readers.* New York: The MacMillan Company, 1952.

Mackay, Charles. *Extraordinary Popular Delusions and the Madness of Crowds.* Reprint. New York: Barnes & Noble Books, 1989.

Marcel Proust, *Remembrance of Things Past: The Captive, The Fugitive, Time Regained.* New York: Vintage Books, 1982.

Murray, Margaret. *The Witch Cult in Western Europe.* Reprint. London: Oxford University Press, 1967.

Näyhä, Simo. "Traffic Deaths and Superstitions on Friday the 13th," *American Journal of Psychiatry,* Vol. 159 (12), 2002.

New Catholic Encyclopedia. New York: McGraw-Hill Book Company, 1967.

Opie, Iona and Tatem, Moria, eds. *A Dictionary of Superstitions.* London: Oxford University Press, 1990.

Page, James D. *Abnormal Psychology: A Clinical Approach to Psychological Deviants.* New York: McGraw-Hill Book Company, 1947.

Pierre-Jean de Béranger. *Chansons.* Paris, 1842.

Platt, Charles. *Popular Superstitions.* London: Herbert Jenkins, Limited, 1925.

Russell, Bertrand. *Unpopular Essays.* New York: Simon & Schuster, 1950.

Scot, Reginald. *The Discoverie of Witchcraft.* London: William Brome, 1584.

Simpson, Jacqueline. "Margaret Murray: Who Believed Her, and Why?" *Folklore 105,* 1994.

Simpson, Jacqueline and Steve Roud. *A Dictionary of English Folklore.* London: Oxford University Press, 2000.

Smith, Gary. "Scared to Death?" *BMJ: British Medical Journal,* Vol. 325 (7378), 2002.

The Unexplained: Superstitions. VHS documentary. A&E Television Networks, 1998.

Thirteen Club. *Annual Report of the Officers of the Thirteen Club, 1883–1914.* New York: The Club.

Thompson, Harold W. *Body, Boots & Britches.* New York: J. B. Lippincott Company, 1940.

Thompson, Tok. "The Thirteenth Number: then, there/ here and now," *Studia Mythologica Slavica V,* 2002, pp. 145–160.

Tuckerman, Nancy, et al. *The Amy Vanderbilt Complete Book of Etiquette.* New York: Doubleday, 1995.

Vyse, Stuart A. *Believing in Magic: The Psychology of Superstition.* New York: Oxford University Press, 2000.

Watkin, David. *A History of Western Architecture.* New York: Barnes & Noble Books, 1996.

Wegrocki, H. J. "A Case of Number Phobia," *International Journal of Psycho-Analysis,* 19, 1938.

Acknowledgments

I WOULD LIKE TO thank all the people who responded to my questionnaire about unlucky 13. I would also like to thank the following individuals, companies, and organizations for their assistance with this book: Airbus, Air Force Historical Research Agency, Scott Alexander, American Film Institute, American Hotel & Lodging Association, American Psychiatric Publishing, Mark Anania, Michele Anderson, Aquila Books, Arizona Lottery, Katherine Austin, Bank One Media Relations, Beth Bass, Joe Bertagna, Boeing, Caryl Burtner, Cafe Literati, Danie Caro, Maryann Ceriello, The Chicago Historical Society, Marcia Choquette, Mary Clutts, Continental Airlines, Crowing Hen

Designs, Cultural Awareness International, Inc., Peter B. Dannenfelser II, Margie DeBolt, Dog Eared Books, Early English Books Online Text Creation Partnership, Eaton Consulting Group, E/C Engineering, Inc., Greg Evans, Frederico Augusto Garcia Fernandes, Dr. Thomas J. Fernsler, Mark G. Fischman, Bryan Fitzgerald, George Eastman House, Elaine Gregory, Kathy Hanpa, Dr. Vanessa Harding, Dr. John C. Hirsh, Cameron Howell, Ibis Books, IMDB.com, Indiana Historical Society, Indiana State Library, Janko Rasic Associates, Richard J. Kaplan, Peter Kassen, David King, Larry Kennan, Patrick Lau, Ari Lehman, Kinda S. Lenberg, Dr. John Lindow, Claude A. Luttrell, Clare MacMahon, Robert T. Matschulat, Matthews International Corporation, Victor Miller, Missouri Lottery, Mitsubishi Electric & Electronics USA, Inc., Eva Llamas Mogan, Mickey Morris, Navy Department Library, Simo Näyhä, New Mexico Lottery Authority, The North Carolina Collection Gallery, Sue Nottingham, Alissa Overend, Victor Pei, Johannes Persson, PECentral.org, Stephen Porter, Protocol & Diplomacy International, Dilip Rangnekar, Alcus Riley, Peter Roth, Ev Ruffcorn, Tom Schier, Schindler Elevator, Ltd., Seatguru.com, Will Shortz, Dr. Margarida de Souza-Neves, Dr. Donca Steriade, Sterling Books, T. R. McTeer, Dr. Tok Freeland Thompson, ThyssenKrupp Elevator, Vermont Lottery, William Reese Company, Patrick Wilson, Joy Woog, Zimmer Gunsul Frasca Partnership, and Keith Zucker.

In addition, I would like to thank the foreign embassies of the following countries, which were kind enough to provide information on number superstitions in their respective cultures: Argentina, Australia, Austria, Belarus, Belgium, Belize, Bolivia,

Brazil, Bulgaria, Canada, Chile, China, Costa Rica, Croatia, Cuba, Czech Republic, Denmark, Ecuador, El Salvador, Estonia, Fiji, Finland, France, Georgia, Germany, Guatemala, Hungary, Iceland, Indonesia, Ireland, Japan, Korea, Lebanon, Lithuania, Mexico, The Netherlands, New Zealand, Norway, Pakistan, Peru, Philippines, Poland, Portugal, Romania, Russia, Saudi Arabia, South Africa, Spain, Sweden, and Switzerland.

I would especially like to thank John G. H. Oakes and Jofie Ferrari-Adler at Thunder's Mouth Press for their commitment and dedication.

Most of all, I would like to thank my family. Stanley, for enduring his demotion from assistant to cat with feline grace and dignity. My mother, for the feedback, the leftovers, and the emergency babysitting. My wife, for being so tirelessly supportive and encouraging—and for giving birth to my new assistant, Arlo, who kept me motivated (and exhausted) every step of the way. Thank you, Rabbit King! I hope that when you are older you will enjoy reading this as much as I enjoyed writing it.

Index